Lincoln Township Public Library
2099 W. John Beers Rd.
Stevensville. MI 49127

D1317807

OWLS

0 11557 03213 0

OWLS

Lincoln Township Public Library
2099 W. John Beers Rd.
Stevensville, MI 49127
(269) 429-9575

Cynthia Berger

illustrations by Amelia Hansen

STACKPOLE
BOOKS

Copyright © 2005 by Cynthia Berger

Published by
STACKPOLE BOOKS
5067 Ritter Road
Mechanicsburg, PA 17055
www.stackpolebooks.com

All rights reserved, including the right to reproduce this book or portions thereof in any form or by any means, electronic or mechanical, including photocopying, recording, or by any information storage and retrieval system, without permission in writing from the publisher. All inquiries should be addressed to Stackpole Books, 5067 Ritter Road, Mechanicsburg, Pennsylvania 17055.

Printed in China

10 9 8 7 6 5 4 3 2 1

First edition

Cover design by Caroline Stover
Illustrations by Amelia Hansen
All photographs by Ron Austing except as follows:
  page 58, top left, Maslowski Wildlife Productions
  page 74, Noel Snyder

Library of Congress Cataloging-in-Publication Data

Berger, Cynthia.
    Owls / Cynthia Berger ; illustrations by Amelia Hansen.— 1st ed.
        p.   cm. — (Wild guide)
    Includes bibliographical references.
    ISBN 0-8117-3213-4
    1. Owls.   2. Owls—North America.   I. Title.   II. Series.
QL696.S83B47   2005
598.9'7'097—dc22

                                                                                2005002317
ISBN 978-0-8117-3213-0

CONTENTS

ACKNOWLEDGMENTS

I am deeply indebted to Dr. James Duncan, the technical editor for this book. Jim is a Canadian wildlife biologist and owl researcher who works for the Wildlife and Ecosystem Protection Branch of Manitoba Conservation as manager of the Biodiversity Conservation Section; he is also the author of a magnificent book, *Owls of the World*. To answer my questions about owl behavior, Jim dug into a personal collection of digital photographs that is quite amazing. His sense of humor and boundless enthusiasm for the subject helped to sustain my own enthusiasm over the course of the project. And his detailed and thoughtful feedback on the illustrations and text have improved both immensely. (Any inadvertent errors or omissions that remain are entirely the fault of the author.)

I also owe heartfelt thanks to another Canadian owl expert, Dr. Robert Nero, who also provided feedback on the text. Bob Nero is famous not only for his research accomplishments but for his lyrical nature books, including three about gray owls. I am honored to have had his input on this work.

Special thanks to Mark Allison, my editor at Stackpole Books, for his ongoing enthusiasm and encouragement, and to Joyce Bond for sensitive and intelligent editing. Illustrator Amelia Hansen has created images that are carefully researched and painstakingly accurate, that perfectly complement the text—and that are breathtaking works of art.

I credit my parents for sparking my lifetime love of nature by taking their young family on so many summer camping trips. And my husband, Bill Carlsen, is a constant source of encouragement. He keeps my electronic cottage stocked with up-to-date technology; he wakes me up on winter nights if he hears owls hooting in the nearby woods; and he knows how to draw owls closer by imitating their calls. For all of these talents and more, I am deeply grateful.

INTRODUCTION

"I rejoice that there are owls."
—Henry David Thoreau

In the spring of 1967, civil defense officials in the Pacific Northwest were startled to receive reports that space aliens had landed in a remote, densely wooded area. Callers said a strange, repetitious beeping signal was emanating from a hilltop. Apparently, the sound started up like clockwork at eight o'clock each evening and continued—constant in pitch and frequency—until four each morning. UFO enthusiasts who hiked in by night to hear the sound reported that a disc-shaped object could sometimes be spotted floating over the hilltop. Police officers were sent in to check these reports, along with some Federal Aviation Administration employees. All of them confirmed the civilian observations.

So there the matter stood, until an investigative team was brought in to record the alien sounds and analyze them. True believers scoffed at what the experts concluded. But the truth was confirmed a few nights later, when a farmer hiked up the hill, aimed his shotgun at the sound, and fired . . . bringing a Northern Saw-whet Owl tumbling to the ground.

This wasn't the first—or the last—time an owl had been mistaken for a UFO. Owls fly at night, they float silently through the air, they make strange noises—and they inspire in the human breast the simultaneous sensations of fear and awed fascination. It's not surprising that some people's minds have turned to space aliens.

Across time and across cultures, we humans have always had a special relationship with owls. Perhaps it's their almost human faces, their often tame and approachable nature, or their haunting voices, but owls naturally capture our imagination—and they always have. One of the earliest examples of a work of art is instantly recognizable as a Long-eared Owl, scratched on the wall of a cave in France more than thirty thousand years ago. No one knows the symbolic importance of this particular image, but since the beginning of recorded human history, humans have identified these night-flying birds with the underworld. The Sumerians of ancient Mesopotamia, who invented writing, left behind a tablet dating to about 2300 BC depicting Lilitu, the goddess of death—a winged woman with feet like an owl's talons, a crown resembling an owl's ear tufts, and two owls for companions. Her name is derived from an ancient word meaning "night."

Cultures that followed the Sumerians continued the tradition of an owl-like death goddess. The Jewish Tanakh (known to Christians as the Old Testament), completed around 700 BC, includes the Hebrew word *lilith*, usually translated as "screech owl"; scholars believe this name evolved from that of the Babylonian goddess. Commentators who interpreted the Tanakh wrote about a woman named Lilith who was Adam's first wife—his partner before Eve was created from his rib. Lilith is described as an assertive and demanding woman who declined to be subservient to Adam and ultimately left him to mate with a demon; according to tradition, she herself became a demon of the night.

The ancient Greeks also had a goddess associated with owls. Pallas Athene, or Athena—a warrior goddess and the goddess of wisdom—had the power to see in the dark, and her symbol and familiar was the owl. The Greek ruler Agathokles of Syracuse is said to have defeated the Carthaginians in 310 BC by capitalizing on the connection between owls and the warrior goddess. As the story goes, he captured a large number of owls, then released them over his assembled troops. The birds, looking for perching posts, settled on the men's helmets and shields, giving them the confidence to win the day.

The Romans held on to many Greek beliefs and customs, and their goddess of wisdom, Minerva, was also associated with an owl. But overall they took an even darker view of owls than the Greeks did. A bird that could see in the dark could also, they believed, predict approaching deaths. The Romans also started the practice of using owl parts in medicines and magic potions; this custom persisted into the Middle Ages in Europe and is also seen in parts of Asia today. Meanwhile, as time marched on, the owl came to be a symbol of evil to the early Christians. Some Roman carvings of the time show Jews as owls being mobbed by flocks of doves or sparrows symbolizing Christians.

The idea that owls are bad omens and can predict an impending death is found in the works of Shakespeare, who has influenced so much of Western literature. In *Macbeth*, for example, the playwright tells us that an owl is a "fatal bellman, which gives the stern'st good-night."

This idea is not unique to the Western world, however. Tribes in northeastern India also believed that when owls called, it meant someone was going to die; in much the same vein, aborigines in northern Australia believed that if an owl hung around a home for a few days, it was warning of a death in the family. In China long ago, villagers believed that a hooting owl was telling people to start digging a grave for someone who was about to die. The ancient Mayans believed an owl hooting loudly for a long time was a bad omen. And various Native American groups, ranging from the Navajo in the Southwest to the Kwakiutl of British Columbia, associate owls with the soul after death.

If the sight or sound of an owl sparks a shiver of fear, owls have paradoxically sustained their reputation as wise birds—a reputation probably developed in Roman times, when scholars stayed up late, studying. If you doubt that this idea still holds today, just cruise the gift-card aisle and count all the graduation cards that show owls wearing mortarboards.

Of course, owls are neither evil nor wise—they are simply birds. As predators at the top of the food chain, they play an important role in ecosystems. A pair of owls who are feeding a clutch of chicks may take more than a thousand mice over the course of a summer, so their presence can be a boon to farmers. In modern times, the fear of owls is fading as people understand that these birds are not harbingers of doom or witches' familiars—they are majestic and beautiful wild animals, perfectly adapted for their role as night-flying hunters.

Worldwide, there are about 205 different species of owls. (We have to say "about" because taxonomists don't agree as to whether certain kinds are full species or subspecies.) This means that, as a group, owls make up a fair-sized subset of the nine thousand or so different species of birds on Earth. Owls are more diverse than, say, herons or cranes (with one or two dozen species apiece) but less diverse than hummingbirds or doves (with about three hundred species apiece) or finches (with more than four hundred).

Either eighteen or nineteen different owl species (depending on what you define as a species) can be found breeding in North America—if you look in all the right places. This book is an introductory guide for anyone who is interested in North American owls and would like to know more about their haunts and habits. Here you'll find information about owl anatomy and behavior—how owls navigate at night, how they hunt, what they eat, where they live, how they find mates and care for their young. This book also includes a field guide to North American species. There are tips for finding and identifying owls in the wild. And you'll learn how you can attract owls to nest in your backyard.

1

What Makes an Owl?

The midday calm of a forest is shattered by agitated bird calls. A little flock of songbirds—chickadees, titmice, and kinglets, all foraging together—has been working its way through the pines. One of the birds has spotted a Great Horned Owl dozing on its daytime perch high in a tree, and now the members of the flock have switched from peaceful chirping to peevish, scolding sounds. Some of the little birds actually attack. They take turns dive-bombing the owl, trying to drive it from their neighborhood.

Songbirds seem to instinctively recognize an owl-like shape—and to know that it represents danger. Researchers who tested this idea found that if they set a chunky, rounded, mottled-brown form out on a perch, the little birds went nuts. This behavior—reacting to anything even vaguely owl-like—is an adaptive response, as owls often catch and eat small songbirds.

Their big round heads, upright posture, and large forward-facing eyes make owls distinctive in appearance and easy to recognize. Other distinctive traits include their sensitive ears, soft feathers for silent flight, powerful beaks, and sharp talons—traits that make them expert hunters and a threat to little songbirds.

Let's take a closer look at these special traits—at what makes an owl an owl.

Keen Vision

Dogs experience the world as a collection of smells. Bats navigate with sonar. Birds are mostly visual creatures. They rely on their eyesight for flying—to orient and maneuver. A blindfolded bird cannot fly. Indeed, birds rely on their vision for most of life's essentials: to find food, shelter, and nest

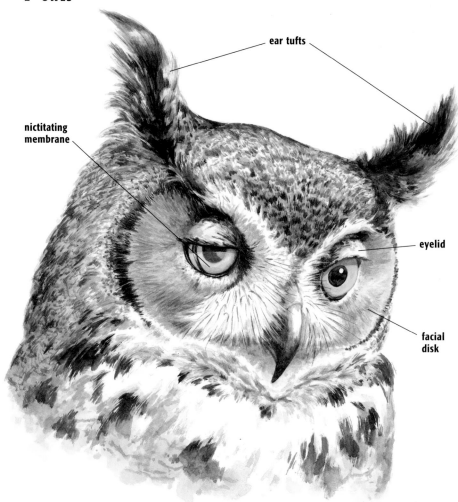

The ear tufts atop this Great Horned Owl's head are not used for hearing—they're just tufts of feathers. The real ears are on the sides of the head, under the feathers of the facial disk. Also notice the "third eyelid" or nictitating membrane, caught in mid-blink.

sites; to navigate; to identify prospective mates and rivals; and to spot potential predators.

Of all the world's birds, owls have especially good eyesight in dim light—though it's just a myth that owls can see in absolute darkness. The way eyes work, at least some light must strike the retina in order for an image to form. Owls do, however, have a remarkable ability to see in what looks to us like pitch darkness. To understand how an owl's eyes work so well at night, it helps to understand, in general, how eyes work:

- Light passes through the transparent *cornea,* the tough outer covering of the eye, and then through the *lens* of the eye.

- The lens focuses light on the *retina,* a thin membrane at the back of the eye.
- Light-sensitive cells cover the retina. *Rod cells* work well in low-light conditions and are very sensitive to black and gray. *Cone cells* work well in bright light and are used to see colors.
- The *optic nerve* is at the back of the eye, behind the retina. It carries information from the retina to the brain, which interprets these signals to form an image.
- The *iris,* the colored part of the eye, is located in front of the lens. Like the diaphragm on a camera, it controls how much light enters the eye.
- The *pupil* is an opening in the iris that admits light. Muscles in the iris contract to make the pupil smaller so it lets in less light, or relax to make the pupil bigger so it lets in more light.

The eyes of all vertebrate animals—birds, reptiles, fish, amphibians, and mammals—have these same structural features: cornea, lens, retina, iris, and pupil. In owls, these features are adapted to provide good vision in low-light conditions.

An owl's pupils can open very wide. If you were standing next to an owl in a forest at night and an optician equipped with a red light came along to measure, he'd find the owl's pupils open far wider than yours. The wider the pupils open, the more light can enter.

The composition of the iris also differs. Humans have smooth muscle in the iris, and this kind of muscle contracts slowly. This means that when light conditions change suddenly, your eyes take time to adjust. When you leave a dark room to walk outside on a sunny day, your eyes are dazzled and you have to squint. In contrast, the irises of owls, like all birds, have striated muscle, which contracts quickly. This means that an owl's eyes adapt faster to changing light conditions, aiding them in navigating through dark forests and across bright moonlit fields.

Another way owl vision is fine-tuned is that the two pupils can open and close independently of one another. Human pupils, in contrast, always work

THE LARGE EYES OF OWLS

Owls have big eyes for their size. Indeed, the eyes take up most of the space inside the owl's skull, and there's not much room left for the brain.

To better appreciate just how large an owl's eyes are, look in the mirror. Notice that when you look at your own eyes, you see both the iris, the colored part of the eye, and the sclera, the white part. Now look at the picture of the owl on the previous page. Notice that only the iris is visible. The white part of the eye is concealed, inside the head. If your eyes were as large in proportion to your head as an owl's eyes are, they'd look like two grapefruits crammed inside your skull!

in tandem. Turn the dimmer switch in the dining room, and as it gets darker, both of your pupils open the exact same amount. Turn the lights up, and your two pupils shrink the exact same amount. Indeed, if you suffer a blow to the head, the doctor will check the size of your pupils, because in humans, pupils that are different sizes are a sign of a brain injury. An owl's pupils, on the other hand, respond independently to light conditions in the environment. It is normal for an owl to have one pupil larger than the other. If the light is a little brighter on one side than on the other, the two eyes adjust perfectly to the conditions around each eye.

Perhaps the most important factor contributing to an owl's excellent night vision is the composition of the retinas. The retinas are covered with two kinds of cells: rods and cones. The retinas of day-flying birds have more cone cells, which are used to perceive colors in bright light. Most day-active birds use color as a cue to find food, identify members of the same species, and pick out mates. Humans also have more cones than rods.

An owl's retinas are very different from the average bird's, and from yours, having far more rods than cones. In some owl species, the retinas are crammed with almost a million rod cells per square millimeter. To put that in perspective, we humans have one-fifth as many, with two hundred thousand rod cells per square millimeter of retina. And remember, rod cells are the ones that respond in dim light.

Not only do owls have lots of rod cells per unit of surface area, but they also have lots of surface area, because they have very large eyes for their size. The average Great Horned Owl, which stands less than 3 feet tall, has eyes as big as those of a full-grown man standing 6 feet tall. The larger the eye, the more cells can fit on the retina. And the more cells on the retina, the more detailed an image an eye can resolve.

Still another factor contributing to an owl's keen vision is the shape of the eyeball itself. An owl's eyes aren't really ball-shaped. They are more like cylinders or tubes—long from front to back, shorter from side to side. This means that the lens is comparatively far from the retina, giving the eye a long focal length. That's excellent for distance vision. Think of an owl's eyes as analogous to high-powered binoculars. They offer a small field of view but a detailed image of objects far away.

An owl's optic nerves carry messages to the brain faster than a human's nerves do. This rapid transmission means that owls are very good at detecting and reacting to even very slight movements in the undergrowth.

For owls, one consequence of having large eyes crammed into a small skull is that there's no room for muscles that rotate the eyes in their sockets. So an owl can't roll its eyes, like a human can; it can only look straight ahead. To see things that are off to one side, the owl has to move its whole head. Luckily, an owl's neck is up to the job—it's long and flexible, with fourteen vertebrae compared with just seven bones in a human neck.

Maybe it sounds strange to assert that owls are long-necked. With so many fluffy feathers around their necks, and with their habit of resting in a hunched

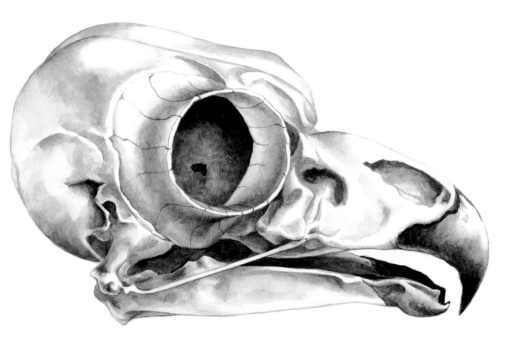

This is the skull of a Great Horned Owl. Notice the sclerotic ring—the bony structure that surrounds the eye. Owl eyes are shaped more like cylinders than like balls—a design that makes vision sharper. But in part because of the bony supporting structure, the eye can't rotate in its socket.

posture, owls look very short-necked. If you check out an owl skeleton, though, you'll see that an owl's neck is surprisingly swanlike.

To see how a long, flexible neck can compensate for eyeball rolling, try this exercise: Hold your shoulders still, look straight ahead, and turn your head to the left as far as it will go. Move only your head—keep your eyes fixed as if you were an owl. Then do the same thing to the right. You can manage about a 90-degree turn in each direction—about a 180-degree field of view in all.

An owl performing the same maneuver can twist its head far beyond 90 degrees to the right or left. It can start out facing forward and end up facing backward (see the Burrowing Owl illustration on the next page). That flexible neck gives an owl a 360-degree field of view. Not only that, but an owl's neck is so flexible that it can even bend its head to the side and keep on bending, turning its head upside down.

Maybe you've heard that owls can spin their heads completely around, like the girl in *The Exorcist*. Indeed, some people once believed you could kill an owl by walking around and around the tree where it was perched; they thought the owl would continue to turn its head until it wrung its own neck. But it's just a myth that owls can spin their heads around. It just looks like they can—kind of an optical illusion.

What owls actually do is swivel their heads really fast. They turn far to the right, then quickly reverse direction, turning far to the left. It all happens so quickly that if you blink, you'll miss the reversal—and you'll swear that the head just spun completely around.

Both owls and humans have binocular vision, with two eyes on the front of the head rather than one eye on each side. With binocular vision, each eye sees the same scene at the same time, though from a slightly different angle. This arrangement provides a three-dimensional view of the world.

Most other birds have monocular vision, with the eyes on opposite sides of the head. One eye looks left, the other right, each seeing a different scene. There's a little overlap in what the two eyes see—each sees a bit of the view directly in front of the bird—but not much. Monocular vision is an aid in scanning for predators. Woodcocks are champions at monitoring their environment; the average woodcock, sitting perfectly still, without moving its head, can see what's going on almost a full 360 degrees around it. But there are drawbacks to monocular vision. For one thing, it doesn't allow for much depth perception; to the average bird, the world appears flat, two-dimensional. And it's hard for birds with monocular vision to judge distances. To do so, they must move their heads, so they can see the same scene with first one eye, then the other.

With binocular vision, owls have excellent depth perception and can judge distances very accurately. That's useful for navigating in the complex environment of a forest—finding perches and avoiding colliding with branches—and for scanning for rodents and other prey from a high perch. And because owls don't need to move their heads as much as most birds, they are less conspicuous and avoid being detected by their prey—or by predators.

If their forward-facing eyes give owls a human appearance, the ability to deliver a genuine wink adds to the illusion. Owls close their eyes by lowering the top eyelids—a skill fairly unusual among birds. Most birds blink by raising the bottom eyelids up. (Parrots, toucans, and ostriches are among the few other groups that have a top-down blink.)

For routine blinking, owls don't use their regular eyelids. They blink with a thin, semitransparent membrane called the nictitating membrane. All birds have this third eyelid (see page 2); it's not unique to owls. The membrane slides diagonally across the eye, from the inside corner to the outside. It keeps the eye surface moist and free of annoying particles and germs.

An owl uses its upper eyelids only when it is settling down to sleep or doze, or when its eyes need extra protection, such as when scratching its face with a claw, snatching prey, or handing off a mouse, beak-to-beak, to a mate or chick. A pair of owls will also close their eyes when preening each other's faces or when copulating.

It may look as if this Burrowing Owl has eyes in the back of its head. Actually, it merely has an extraordinarily flexible neck—as do all owls.

Sharp Hearing

It's just a myth that owls can see in absolute darkness. Remember, the cells on the retina must be stimulated by photons of light for the eye to resolve an image. In the absence of light, owls can't see a thing. Just the same, some owls can catch mice in a pitch black room. They do it by following prey with their ears.

A scientist named Roger Payne discovered this when he conducted landmark studies of hearing in Barn Owls almost half a century ago. At the time, Payne was a graduate student at Cornell University. He started by training Barn Owls to catch mice in a windowless room, leaving the lights on. Then he spread dry leaves on the floor, turned the lights out so that the room was completely dark, and released some more mice. Though they couldn't see their prey, the owls caught the mice handily.

This result suggested that the owls were locating mice by ear alone. But there were other possible explanations. One idea was that owls were smelling their way to the prey. Most birds have a poor sense of smell, however. Another idea was that the barn owls were homing in on warm little bodies in a cold room. Night-hunting snakes use infrared sensors to detect a mouse's body heat; perhaps owls had the same ability.

Payne modified his experiment to test these ideas. He crumpled up some wads of paper, tied them to strings, and tied the strings to the tails of some more experimental mice. When he released the mice in the room, the paper wads dragged noisily through the dry leaves. This time, when the barn owls attacked, they aimed for—and caught—the paper, not the mice. This showed that the owls were targeting sounds, not heat or smell; otherwise they would have caught the mice.

Owls rely on their sense of hearing for more than just zeroing in on prey. Active at night, owls depend on audible signals—hoots or screams—to attract mates or to defend territories. Owls also rely on their sense of hearing to stay in touch with their mates and owlets, which hang around with their parents for weeks to months after leaving the nest.

Not all owls have equally adept ears. The species that hunt almost exclusively at night or that hunt hidden prey by day have the most sensitive hearing. Other species that hunt by day rely more on their eyes and less on their ears, and their hearing is not as acute.

The design and placement of an owl's ears contribute to its excellent hearing. Humans have conspicuous outer ears, as do most mammals. Our skin-covered flaps of cartilage, called auricles, work like miniature satellite dishes to focus sounds toward the ear openings.

Owls, like all birds, don't have auricles sticking out from the sides of their heads. Birds are designed for flight, and big ear flaps would not be aerodynamic. Typically, a bird's ear openings, called apertures, are just little round holes in the sides of the head. To see the apertures, you'd have to hold the bird in your hand and push the feathers aside.

An owl's ear apertures are covered by specialized feathers—the feathers of the facial disk. Round or heart-shaped, this concave bowl of feathers does the same job as your auricles, working like a parabolic dish to funnel sound waves into the ears.

Don't all those fluffy feathers interfere with hearing? After all, on other parts of the body, feathers act as insulation, and insulation tends to dampen sounds. Actually, the feathers over an owl's ears work more like the mesh that covers a stereo speaker than like a roll of egg-carton padding on a studio wall. Sounds pass right through the feathers.

Most feathers are fluffy along their entire length, but feathers in the facial disk are fluffy just at the tips; they're almost bare along the length of the shaft. This creates gaps, like the holes in stereo-speaker mesh that admit sound

EAR TUFTS

At first glance, a Great Horned Owl resembles a cat. It has big eyes in a round face, a triangular beak that looks similar to a cat's flat nose, and what might be mistaken for perky ears on top of its head.

These structures are called ear tufts, but the name is misleading. Although they look like ears, they are just bunches of feathers that stick up. They are not connected to the owl's actual ears and have absolutely nothing to do with its ability to hear. An owl's real ears are on the sides of its head, hidden under the feathers of the facial disk.

Not all owls have ear tufts. Some, such as pygmy-owls and Burrowing Owls, have smooth, round heads. Flammulated and Short-eared Owls have small, inconspicuous ear tufts. North American owls with large, easy-to-see ear tufts include the Great Horned Owl, both the Eastern and Western Screech-Owls, and the Long-eared Owl.

The feathers that make up an ear tuft are controlled by small muscles under the skin. An owl can use these muscles to make its ear tufts stand up straight or fold almost flat. When an owl folds its ear tufts flat, it looks round-headed, which can be confusing for bird-watchers who are trying to make an ID based on whether the owl has ear tufts.

If ear tufts aren't actually ears, what good are they? Scientists aren't sure, but they have some ideas. One is that ear tufts are part of an owl's camouflage system. Tufts break up the broad, smooth outline of the head, helping owls blend in against a background of jagged-edged leaves and furrowed tree bark. Another idea is that ear tufts create a distinctive shape so that members of the same species can recognize one another in dim light. Still another theory holds that ear tufts have defensive value. Maybe erect ear tufts make an owl look bigger and more formidable. Or maybe predators back off because an owl with erect ear tufts looks like a ferocious lynx or a bobcat.

It does seem clear that an owl's ear tufts are expressive—that their movements reflect the owl's emotions. An owl that is alert and relaxed will hold its ear tufts erect, much like a dog or a horse that feels happy and secure. An owl that feels threatened or frightened may raise its ear tufts higher still, like a cat with hackles raised, or it may fold its ear tufts flat, like a cat that is about to hiss and claw.

waves. Meanwhile, just as mesh on a speaker protects the delicate speaker components, the feathers protect the ears, keeping out dust and dirt and preventing injury while the owl maneuvers among sharp twigs or tussles with prey that bites back.

The feathers of the facial disk are arranged in a shallow, concave bowl that probably works like a satellite dish, amplifying sounds by focusing them toward the ear openings. With this built-in amplifier, owls can detect faint sounds that humans cannot hear at all.

Owls that fly only at night tend to have large facial disks with a well-defined edge. Owls that are active by day and rely more on vision have smaller and less clearly defined facial disks. In a 1970s study, a researcher experimented with removing feathers from the facial disks of some Barn Owls. Like the biblical Samson, who lost his legendary strength after a haircut, the Barn Owls lost some of their hunting skills after the feather trim and tended to land short of their targets.

Muscles under the skin let an owl move the feathers of the facial disk to change its shape and improve its ability to catch sound waves. The rearmost feathers in the disk, called the ruff feathers, are also movable.

Under those feathers, day-flying owls that are visual hunters have small, round apertures, or ear openings. Night-flying owls, as well as day flyers that hunt concealed prey, such as Great Gray Owls and Boreal Owls, tend to have very large ear apertures. In some species, the apertures are vertical slits that run almost the entire length of the head; for example, the Long-eared Owl's ear apertures start above each eye and extend down to the chin region. The ear parts inside the head are also oversize in owls. The outer ear tube is wide, and the inner ear is very large for the bird's size.

In some owl species, the aperture is protected by one or two skin flaps. Such an ear flap is called an operculum, the same word used for the hard flap over a fish's gills or the flap that a snail uses to seal its shell. Like these opercula, an owl's operculum is movable—it can be pulled flat against the ear aperture or stand out from the owl's head. Movements of the opercula can change the shape of the facial disk. There's also some evidence that owls use these flaps like auxiliary satellite dishes, to focus or direct sound waves coming from different directions.

It's not just the size of an owl's ear apertures that is important for good hearing. Where these openings are placed on the head also contributes to hearing ability. Take a look at the illustration of the Boreal Owl skull on the next page. Like all owls, this species has a comparatively large and wide head for its size. This means that for its size, its ears are set comparatively far apart. This wide-set arrangement helps the owl tell where a sound is coming from.

To understand why this is so, think of an owl that has alighted on the ground. A mouse is rustling in the grass off to its left. The sound waves travel toward the owl, and they enter the owl's left ear just a fraction of a second before they hit the right ear. Not only does the timing differ, but the sound will be a tiny bit louder in the left ear than in the right ear.

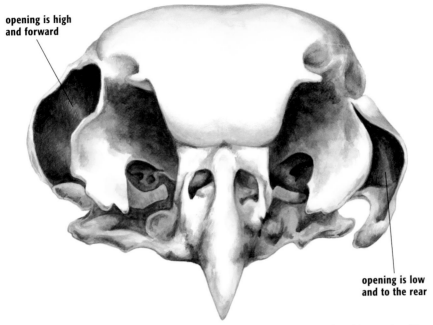

opening is high and forward

opening is low and to the rear

The skull of a Boreal Owl appears misshapen, but this is normal for this species. The unequal ear openings (one placed high and forward on the skull, one placed low and to the rear) are an adaptation that improves the owl's ability to locate prey by sound alone.

Scientists think that the owl's brain automatically processes and compares the sounds from the two ears and translates that information into a unified perception—an understanding of where the sound is coming from. All animals with two ears can make this calculation; it's just that owls are especially good at it.

Typically, a sound that is coming from an owl's far left side will reach its left ear about two hundred microseconds before it reaches the right ear. The owl's brain is up to this challenge, however: It can perceive a time difference as small as ten to thirty microseconds. Scientists who have studied the brain structure of owls say that the medulla, the part that interprets sounds, is very large. An owl's medulla contains three times as many neurons as the medullas of most other birds.

Responding to its powerful brain's lightning-fast calculations, the owl uses a process called triangulation, turning its head until the sound arrives simultaneously in both ears. Now it is directly facing its prey.

Owls most often hunt from a perch, or sometimes while flying. This means they need to be able to identify where a sound is coming from not just in a two-dimensional plane, but in three dimensions. They must determine whether the sound is coming from left or right, front or back, and above or below.

The placement of an owl's ears facilitates this three-dimensional hearing. In contrast to a human's ears, which are symmetrical, an owl's ears may be

TRIANGULATION

To understand how triangulation works, picture a triangle with one very short side and two very long sides that are unequal in length, one just a little longer than the other. The short side is the base of the triangle, and the two long sides meet in a sharp point.

Now imagine a mouse at the sharp point of the triangle. The base of the triangle is the distance between the owl's two ears. The long sides trace the distance from each ear to the mouse.

To triangulate on a sound, the owl turns its head. When the two sides of the triangle are equal in length, the sound is arriving at both ears simultaneously and the owl is directly facing its prey. An owl that cannot hear in one ear will not be able to tell where a sound is coming from.

asymmetrical, with apertures of different shapes and sizes, and in different locations on the head.

In general, day-hunting owls have more symmetrical ears, and night-hunting owls have more asymmetrical ears. Boreal Owls have the most asymmetrical ears of any North American owl. Take another look at the Boreal Owl skull. See how it looks almost misshapen? Notice that the right ear opening is larger than the left; the right opening is located higher on the skull than the left; and the right opening is positioned farther forward on the skull than the left.

These differences are what help the owl determine whether a sound is coming from above or below. They allow it to triangulate in three dimensions, not just two. The owl's brain makes these calculations automatically, based on the differences in sounds hitting each ear. Once an owl is lined up on a mouse (this happens much faster than it takes to tell the story), it launches from its perch and flies toward the sound, making quick, small corrections to its flight path to stay on target, because the mouse may be moving too.

Day-hunting owls that go after concealed prey, such as Great Gray Owls, also tend to have very asymmetrical ears. In winter, the favorite prey of Great Grays, voles and mice, live in tunnels under the snow. In the long days of northern summers, the owls hunt by daylight, but their prey is still hidden: mice and voles take cover in the grass, and pocket gophers have underground tunnels. Their asymmetrical ears allow the Great Grays to triangulate on this invisible prey.

Functional Feathers

Owls have sharper eyes and keener ears than most other birds, and these two traits are important for their success as hunters. But there's more in an owl's hunting kit. A suit of feathers is like a hunter's carefully chosen parka and leggings. Feathers afford camouflage, so that an owl can blend with the forest background. They provide warmth and are waterproof in bad weather. And like outerwear made from high-tech fabric, an owl's feathers are quiet.

An owl's feathers are specially adapted for silent flight—note the serrated edge on the primary feather (middle), which reduces turbulence and therefore noise during flight. Owl feathers are also adapted to provide warmth in cold climates; though owls have fewer down feathers (bottom right) than most birds, all of their contour feathers (top left) have a downy base.

A Barn Owl in flight. Notice how wide this owl's wings are compared to its body. Low "wing loading" contributes to an owl's ability to fly silently.

Why is that important? Hunters don't want to startle their prey; they want to be able to sneak close. It's much easier for an owl to catch a rat or mouse when it's calmly standing still rather than running away.

Most birds make noise when they fly. When a flock of pigeons or ducks is startled into flight, not only do they call noisily as they are taking off, but the movement of their wings against the air also makes noise, as does the action of feathers rubbing against one another. The flight feathers of most birds are stiff and hard; in flight, they hit against each other like pieces of stiff plastic, making a clacking noise.

An owl's feathers, on the other hand, are specially modified for silent flight. The upper surfaces of the wing feathers are very soft, with a velvety texture, so they don't make as much noise when they rub against each other. Also, the outermost feather on each wing, called the tenth primary, has an unusual leading edge with little serrations like the teeth of a comb (see page 13). You can see these with the naked eye if you look closely.

Primary feathers are the longest, strongest feathers on the wing and are the most important feathers for flight. Most birds have primary feathers with a stiff leading edge; when it cuts through the air, air rushes up over the wing surface, creating a swirl of turbulence, which makes noise. The serrations on an owl's tenth primary feathers divide the air current, so that instead of one big swirl of turbulence, there are many tiny microturbulences over the wing. The end result is that the wing cuts through the air with much less noise.

The design of an owl's wings also contributes to its ability to fly as quietly as a ghost. A typical owl's wings are large for its body size, and often both broad and rounded. Relative to the owl's overall weight, there's lots of surface area providing lift. An owl is said to have "low wing loading"—it's built more like a glider than a jumbo jet. With low wing loading, owls are very good at quiet gliding; they don't need to do a lot of noisy flapping to get where they are going.

It's easy to see how silent flight benefits a night-hunting owl because of the "sneak up" factor—prey animals don't hear the owl coming, so they don't startle and run away. But silent flight is useful in another way. Night-flying owls rely on their sense of hearing as much as sight to find their prey. By flying quietly, they don't interfere with their own hearing. While in flight, they continuously scan the night soundscape, listening for telltale noises that will help them lock in on a target.

Different owl species are adapted for silent flight to different degrees. Owls that hunt mainly at night, such as Great Horned Owls and screech-owls, have softer feathers than day-active owls, such as Elf Owls, Burrowing Owls, and pygmy-owls.

Snowy Owls, which live on the windy tundra, and Northern Hawk Owls, which live in boreal forests, are two exceptions to the rule that owls have very soft feathers. Quite the opposite—these owls have very stiff feathers that work like a windbreaker worn over a fleece jacket; they cut the wind better than a layer of soft feathers would. These two species often hunt by day and locate their prey visually, so silent flight is less crucial for them.

A Snowy Owl's feathers keep it so warm that during arctic winters, it can continue its daily routine even in extremely low temperatures. Yet owls don't have an insulating layer of fluffy down under their contour feathers like waterfowl do. They stay warm thanks to their modified contour feathers.

Contour feathers are the small, smooth feathers that cover most of a bird's body, giving it a characteristic color and shape. On most birds, the contour feathers are smooth and sleek, the same from tip to base. An owl's contour feathers, however, are like a hybrid between other birds' down feathers and contour feathers. They are smooth at the tip but fluffy at the base.

If you've ever done any winter camping, you know that to stay warm overall, it's essential to keep your feet warm. This rule applies to owls, too: species that live in cold climates have feathers all the way down their legs and over their toes. Foot feathers are more than just cozy; they also seem to work a little bit like antennae or feelers, helping the owl feel for its prey in the dark and protecting its toes from the teeth of rodents that fight back.

An owl's camouflage colors—mostly muted browns and grays—don't really contribute to its hunting prowess, but they do keep the hunter from

MOLTING

A bird's feathers are made mostly of keratin, the same material that makes up your fingernails. Keratin is something of a miracle substance. It's simultaneously flexible, lightweight, very tough, and strong.

Though keratin is tough, over time a bird's feathers can get a bit worn down—from rubbing together in flight, against tree branches in the course of a day's activities, and on the entrance to a nest as the parent bird enters and leaves. Feathers may even break in a fight, in a collision, or while escaping from a predator.

Birds replace their feathers on a regular basis, usually once a year. New feathers work better for flying and keep a bird warmer than raggedy ones. Typically, feathers are replaced at the end of the breeding season, after the young birds have left the nest and become independent, when the parents no longer have to work so hard keeping their offspring fed. The new feathers start to grow, pushing the old feathers out, in a process called molting.

It takes the average bird a few months to molt completely. Owls molt much more slowly. They need to keep flying during the molt, as a flightless owl would starve to death or be taken by a predator. Owls typically replace a few flight feathers one year, a few more the next year, until after about three years all have been replaced. They are never grounded due to repairs.

becoming the hunted. Though all owls are predators, they still have enemies. Large owls will catch and eat smaller ones, and even the big owls have to watch out for eagles and large hawks. Their drab colors and mottled markings help owls blend into the forest background. This is especially important during the day, when most owls find a quiet place where they can roost to sleep or just relax.

Many owls have plumage patterns that perfectly match their habitat. Eastern and Western Screech-Owls have feather markings that make them look like furrowed tree bark. A Snowy Owl's white feathers are nearly invisible against the snow that blankets the tundra most of the year. Short-eared Owls and Burrowing Owls, which nest on the ground, are lighter in color than their forest relatives, allowing them to blend with a background of dry grass.

Predatory Beaks and Talons

Most scientists now agree that owls are most closely related to the night-flying birds called nightjars. But not so long ago, most experts believed that owls should be classified as relatives of hawks, eagles, and falcons. One reason for the old classification system was that owls, like hawks, eagles, and falcons, are predators, and as such carry the same deadly weapons. They have sharp, down-curved beaks, designed for tearing flesh, and very strong feet. The foot bones are thick for their size, and the toes are tipped by curved, needle-sharp talons, perfect for grasping and puncturing prey.

Like most birds, owls have four toes on each foot. But these are rather talented toes. A typical bird's foot has three toes pointing forward and one toe pointing backward. Owls have convertible feet. They can do the three-forward, one-back arrangement, or they can swing the outermost toe backward so that the foot has two toes pointing forward and two pointing backward.

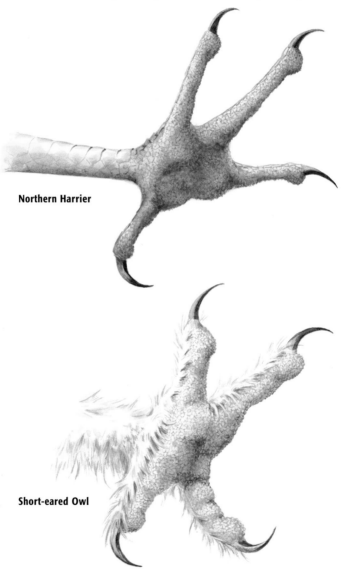

Northern Harrier

Short-eared Owl

Compare the foot of a bird of prey (the Northern Harrier) to the foot of an owl (the Short-eared Owl). Notice that the owl's foot is feathered, has rough bumps for a good grip, and has one toe that swings around so the foot can have two toes forward and two back, widening its grasp when pinning down prey.

This skill comes in handy. An owl that is attacking may leave its perch with its toes in the three-and-one arrangement, but then, as it swings its feet forward to strike, it spreads its toes into the two-and-two configuration. With the toes of each foot spread into the shape of a square rather than a triangle, each foot can cover more surface area, improving the chances that the owl will pin down its target.

Because of the way tendons and muscles are arranged inside the legs, the toes automatically spread wide as the owl straightens its legs to strike its target. When the feet hit the prey and the legs fold on impact, this folding action acts on the flexor tendons, which run up the backs of the ankles, and the toes close automatically. The action drives the talons into soft flesh with fearful force. The blow may be enough to make the kill, especially if the talons puncture vital internal organs.

Owls use the two-and-two toe configuration not just for striking at prey, but also when carrying a carcass in flight or perching on a branch. Whenever the legs bend, the toes curl in, locking onto the prey or wrapping tightly around the branch. This autolock feature is real energy saver, allowing the owl to keep a good grip on its perch without having to continuously contract its muscles. And with the talons locked in place, there's less chance a squirming squirrel will wriggle free. Owls have very rough-soled feet, which also helps them get a good grip. The locking mechanism releases automatically when the owl straightens its legs.

An owl's beak is as sharp as its talons. If you take a close look, you can see that the edges taper like knife edges. When an owl bites down, the upper and lower halves of the beak overlap just a little, like the blades on a pair of kitchen shears, and like kitchen shears they are sharp enough to slice through flesh and bone. If an owl's prey survives the first strike, the bird may deliver the death blow with a bite to the spinal cord at the base of the neck (if the prey is large) or simply by crushing the skull with a bite (if the prey is small).

Most birds have beaks that stick straight out. Because an owl's beak curves downward and its base is hidden by feathers, it looks smaller than it really is. If you happen to come across a barn owl chick in its nest, it's hard to imagine how it could possibly swallow a whole rat, headfirst . . . until that little chick opens wide. At full gape, the broad base of its beak is visible, and rat swallowing seems more plausible.

The curved tip of an owl's beak works like a grappling hook. It's handy both for keeping a grip on carcasses and for tearing into them. Owls usually carry prey in their feet, but they sometimes carry small prey in their hooked bills.

Though owls usually swallow small prey headfirst and whole, they can also use their beaks to dice and serve smaller portions to their chicks, or to carve up a carcass that really is too big to swallow whole, such as a skunk or muskrat. If you're walking in the woods and come across the remains of a kill, look closely. A fox will crunch up the bones and tear the carcass apart. A gleaming skeleton in the woods, neatly picked clean, is probably the work of an owl.

2

Haunts

To set the mood of a movie, Hollywood directors often use bird sounds. The cackle of a Kookaburra tells you something ominous lurks in the jungle; the mewling of gulls adds melancholy to a scene set at the shore; and the mournful hoot of a Great Horned Owl is often a prelude to terror. Even if your face is buried in your companion's shoulder and your eyes are squeezed tight, when you hear the owl, you know what the scene must be—a forest at night, with dappled shadows cast by trees crowded close, their bare, contorted branches tracing patterns against a full moon.

It's a cliché, for sure, yet it's a fair generalization: most species of North American owls spend at least some of their time in a landscape dominated by trees. But this generalization is also a little simplistic. Owls are big birds, and they are predators; they're at the top of the food chain, or close to it. So over evolutionary time, different owl species have adapted to make a comfortable living in many different kinds of places, not just forests.

Almost anywhere in North America that you look, you'll find at least one owl species. Owl habitats range from old-growth forests to young pine plantations, from grasslands to swamps, from deserts to the tundra.

Distribution

Scientists describe where owls (and other animals) live by their distribution and habitat. Distribution is more of a geographic term, indicating a place on a map, a specific region or regions where members of a particular species are known to live. Habitat is defined as "the place where a species usually lives." It may sound as though habitat and distribution mean the same thing, but they actually are somewhat different. Distribution refers to an area on a map; habitat is what you'd see if you actually traveled to the place on the map. Another word for distribution is range. When you plot the distribution of a species on a map, you get a range map.

Although North American birds in general have been well studied, owls as a group have not. As a result, some of the owl range maps you see in field guides have been inked with a pretty broad brush. Not much is known about owls in northern forests. After all, there just aren't that many people up in the north woods—not a lot of enthusiastic bird clubbers volunteering for surveys to find out where owls do and do not live.

Even if the U.S. and Canadian governments were willing and able to deploy an army of scientists or volunteers to study owls in remote places, it's hard to get around in northern forests. There aren't many roads. Winters are long. Temperatures are extreme. The snow is deep. In the summer, insects bite.

So allowing for the possibility that some owl range maps are generous and others are conservative, it's still safe to say that about half of all North American owls are fairly widely distributed, and the others have a more limited distribution.

The Great Horned Owl is the most widely distributed owl species in North America. You can find Great Horned Owls, year-round, almost everywhere except the treeless tundra. This species' range also extends to South America.

Another species that's widely distributed in North America is the Short-eared Owl. It's found in northern and southern areas, eastern and western areas—but only where conditions are right for its hunting habits (it hunts over open grasslands, not in forests). Short-eared Owls also breed in Europe, Asia, and parts of South America.

Barn Owls are the most widely distributed owl species in the world. They're found in the milder climate zones of North America—most of the United States but not Canada. Barn Owls can also be found on every other continent in the world except Antarctica.

Snowy Owls and Northern Hawk Owls aren't widely distributed in North America, but within a global framework you'd say they're widespread. Both species have what's called a circumpolar distribution. Snowies live on the band of tundra that circles the top of the globe; Northern Hawk Owls live in the band of boreal forest just south of this band of tundra. The distribution of both species includes Canada and nations in northern Europe and Asia.

An example of a North American owl with a limited distribution is the Elf Owl. This tiniest of owls breeds only in Mexico and the U.S. states that border it. Then there's the Flammulated Owl, found only in high-elevation western forests of Douglas fir and ponderosa pine.

Whether or not an owl is widely distributed depends on several factors, including where and what it likes to hunt, and what kinds of nest sites it finds acceptable. One reason Great Horned Owls are so widespread is that they are generalists on both of these fronts. Great Horned Owls are known to have tackled hundreds of different kinds of prey: rats and mice, frogs and fish, skunks, domestic cats, geese, and grouse. Wherever a Great Horned Owl chooses to live, it has no trouble getting a meal.

Another reason Great Horned Owls are so ubiquitous is that they're not fussy about their nest sites. A nest made of sticks, abandoned by a crow? A nice big tree hole? A squirrel's nest left over from the previous winter? A handy cave in a cliff face? A ledge in an abandoned barn? All of these make fine nest sites for a Great Horned Owl.

Once a range map is published in a bird guide, we tend to take it for gospel, but a species' distribution is not necessarily fixed. Many North American birds have experienced range expansions in just the past century, with members of the species taking up residence in new places. Other species have experienced the opposite phenomenon, a range contraction, having disappeared from places where they used to live.

Scientists recently documented what looks like a range expansion by two northern owl species, the Boreal Owl and the Northern Hawk Owl, into Nova Scotia, which is located at the far southeastern edge of Canada and was considered to be outside the range of both species. A few individuals had been seen there from time to time but presumably were just wandering vagrants. In 1996, however, birds of both species were spotted nesting and raising chicks in Nova Scotia's Cape Breton Highlands National Park.

Why did these owls move into a new area? An insect pest inadvertently made the place attractive for them. In the 1970s and '80s, spruce budworms—caterpillars that feed on evergreen needles—attacked Nova Scotia's forests. They ate all the needles off a lot of trees. After a few years of defoliation, the trees died; black spruce and balsam fir were especially hard hit. Meanwhile, birch trees were left standing.

So the landscape was transformed from dense forest to sparse woodland. More sunlight was able to reach the forest floor, so shrubs and other low-growing plants flourished. The tangled cover made a great home for mice and other small rodents, and they flourished too. That's when the owls showed up, to feast on the bounty.

The Elf Owl is expanding its range on one front but experiencing a range contraction on another front. Elf Owls that breed in Texas and New Mexico have been moving northward—into the Rio Grande Valley of Texas, into the Guadalupe Mountains and Edwards Plateau, and into the Magdalena Mountains. No one knows why this expansion is under way; one idea is that a warming climate trend has made these northerly areas more hospitable. Meanwhile, Elf Owls have all but disappeared from another part of their breeding range, in southeastern California. Cottonwood trees and mesquite thickets used to border the Colorado River here, but this excellent owl habitat has been cut for firewood, bulldozed to make way for agriculture, or replaced by an exotic plant, salt cedar.

For sheer geographic audacity in the range-expansion department, the Barred Owl takes the cake. Just 150 years ago, this species lived only in the eastern half of the United States. But in the second half of the nineteenth century,

Barred Owls, like hardy pioneers, started heading west. In 1886, they were spotted in southern Manitoba. By 1948, they were in Saskatchewan. By the 1960s, they were on the Pacific Coast. Barred Owls also explored new territory to the south, nesting in California by 1991, and to the north, having recently reached southeast Alaska.

Each individual Barred Owl is rather a stay-at-home. A pair may use the same territory year after year. So how did they manage to spread so far west? Probably through the movements of young owls. Each year in the fall, young owls leave their parents and disperse, moving away from the sites where they were reared to look for territories of their own. Most young owls move just a small distance, but some go far. Over time these movements can add up.

And why were Barred Owls suddenly able to move west, after being confined to the East? One idea is that Great Horned Owls got out of their way. The two species don't always share space comfortably. Great Horned Owls are bigger than Barred Owls—and will eat them. Also, the two species take the same kinds of prey. In some locations, Great Horned Owls seem to prevent Barred Owls from sharing the same patch of forest. There's some evidence that western Great Horned Owl populations have declined in the last century, and it's possible that change allowed Barred Owls to move in.

Another idea is that climate change paved the way for the owls' range expansion. Over the past century, the band of boreal forest that traverses Canada has experienced more rainfall and warmer summer temperatures than in previous centuries, perhaps making conditions more appealing to Barred Owls.

Still another idea is that owls moved west not through the boreal forest, but across the prairies. By suppressing natural prairie fires and planting trees in shelterbelts on farms, settlers may have created a corridor of owl habitat.

These ideas are all intriguing; the challenge is to find sufficient data to support them. There just isn't lot of historic information on Barred Owl distributions.

Habitat

Habitat typically is described in terms of the most common plants present. For example, a forest habitat is dominated by trees; grasses carpet the land in a prairie habitat; cactus is common in a desert habitat. Within each general category, there are more precise categories, such as spruce-fir forest habitat in the West, beech-maple forest habitat in the North, longleaf pine forest habitat in the South.

Habitats may also be defined by their physical or chemical characteristics: high or low elevation; acid or alkaline soil; steep, rolling, or flat terrain. Lakes, rivers, and streams are habitats defined by a shared physical characteristic, water.

Most owls live in forest habitat, but not all do. The largest North American owl species—the ones that mostly prey on birds and mammals—are generally forest species. But the small, insect-eating owls tend to live in dry, open habitats. Short-eared Owls and Burrowing Owls occupy grassland habitat. Snowy Owls and some Short-eared Owls hunt and breed on the treeless tundra.

Some owls can't be pinned down to a single type of habitat. Owls need a place to roost by day, a place to hunt, and in season a place to nest. They may use a different kind of habitat to meet each of these needs. Many owls roost and nest in forest habitat, where dense growth offers protection from predators, then hunt over open habitat, such as a forest clearing, meadow, field, swamp, or marsh.

When several owl species share the same habitat, they may divide up the resources by hunting in slightly different places or at different times of day, taking different sizes of prey, using different nest sites, or some combination of these strategies. One recent study looked at Great Horned Owls, Long-eared Owls, Burrowing Owls, and Barn Owls, all living in the same general area in Colorado. Great Horned Owls, the biggest species, took the biggest prey and hunted mostly at dusk or dawn. Barn Owls and Long-eared Owls hunted only at night, and Burrowing Owls hunted by day as well as night. Barn Owls took heavier prey, mostly voles; Long-ears took lighter prey, mostly mice.

Owls don't always have to split things up this way. In northern areas, certain kinds of prey such as northern voles and lemmings go through regular population cycles. When the cycles are at their peak and the little rodents are superabundant, a number of different owl species can easily share the same habitat, feeding on the same prey in the same places and nesting close together.

Finally, owls that migrate occupy different habitats at different times of year. Most owls, however, do not migrate.

Conservation Issues

Most North American owl species have healthy populations. A few species, however, are officially listed as threatened or endangered, and a few more are considered by the government to be "species of concern." In every case, loss of habitat has been an important factor in bringing the species to its precarious state.

The Northern Spotted Owl, found in the Pacific Northwest and British Columbia, is federally listed as threatened under the U.S. Endangered Species Act and also listed as endangered under the Species at Risk Act in Canada. This species does best in old-growth forests, where most trees are more than 140 years old and some trees are much as 1,000 years old. In the past century, most of the prime Spotted Owl habitat has been clear-cut or selectively logged.

The Spotted Owl's story is a controversial one. Some researchers assert that these owls must have old-growth forests to survive; others point to evidence suggesting that they may be able manage in younger forests. Complicating the question of habitat loss is the fact that Barred Owls have expanded their range into Spotted Owl habitat over the last four decades. Bigger and more aggressive, the Barred Owls may be contributing to Spotted Owl declines by evicting them from the area. Barred Owls and Spotted Owls also interbreed, and hybridizing could mean fewer "purebred" Spotted Owls in the population. Still, it seems hard to deny that clear-cutting vast tracts of forest must be a factor in this shy owl's decline.

Then there's the Cactus Ferruginous Pygmy-Owl, a subspecies of the Ferruginous Pygmy-Owl, which is common in Mexico and South America. The "Cactus" version, which is found only in Arizona and Texas, was listed as endangered in the United States in 1997. It is all but extinct in southern Arizona, where suburban sprawl from fast-growing Tucson has expanded into the owl's Sonoran Desert habitat of saguaro cactus and ironwood. As of 2004, developers were challenging the endangered listing.

Burrowing Owls, listed as endangered in Canada and Mexico, are also considered a species of concern at the federal level in the United States and listed as endangered in Minnesota, threatened in Colorado, and as a species of concern in California, Montana, Oklahoma, Oregon, Utah, Washington, and Wyoming. Once again, the problem is habitat loss. Burrowing Owls require grassland habitat. Since European settlement, the United States and Canada have lost most of their grasslands to farming—and most of the rest to suburbanization.

Elf Owls are listed as endangered in California, which is the northernmost boundary of their breeding range. In the part of California where they are found, the Colorado River has been dammed and redirected to meet the needs of agriculture—and along the way, most of the Elf Owl's habitat has been eliminated. Is this story starting to get a bit repetitive?

Among other owl species that face challenges because of habitat loss, the Short-eared Owl is a species of concern in Canada and a migratory nongame bird of management concern in the United States. Many Short-eared Owls nest on grasslands (others nest farther north on arctic prairies), and North America's grasslands have been mostly replaced with farm fields. Meanwhile, the Flammulated Owl is on the National Audubon Society's watchlist because the western ponderosa pine forests it relies on are being logged.

One widespread twentieth-century habitat modification that has had an impact on many species of owls is the construction of roads. Roads often have wide shoulders bordered with tall grasses or shrubs—perfect habitat for small rodents. And roads often have overhanging trees—perfect places for owls to sit and scan for prey. The problem is that owls, when they're hunting, are very single-minded birds. They're extremely focused. They simply don't notice the flash of headlights or the roar of an engine, or realize that an automobile's path is about to coincide with theirs. Uncounted numbers of owls die in collisions with cars each year.

On the other side of the ledger sheet, in just a few cases, humans have changed the landscape in ways that have helped owls. Both Eastern and Western Screech-Owls are finding suburban backyards with mature trees to be perfectly to their liking. The conversion of forests to farmland in the nineteenth and early twentieth centuries also created lots of new habitat for Barn Owls and Long-eared Owls, both of which hunt over grasslands. In the late twentieth century, however, some of that owl habitat disappeared. In many cases, small farms were consolidated into large industrial farms, and the old hedgerows and windbreaks were bulldozed to make room for monster farm machines, eliminating owl perch sites. Other farms have grown back up into forest or have been turned into housing developments, particularly in the eastern United States. The Long-eared Owl, a species of concern in many states, is listed as endangered in Connecticut and threatened in New Jersey because so many farm fields have reverted to forest.

Territoriality

Within the right habitat, where do you find owls? Owls don't cluster like penguins nesting on a rocky shore, or like Canada Geese grazing on a lawn. Usually, each owl—or pair of owls—defends a territory. Other owls, keep out!

Territoriality is a common behavior among birds. Sometimes the area defended is a feeding territory; other times it's a breeding territory. A breeding territory may include just the nest site itself or a larger area centered on the nest site. The Northern Mockingbird is a familiar example of a bird that defends both kinds of territories: a breeding territory in the spring and a feeding territory (often, a berry-loaded bush) in the fall and winter.

Among birds as a group, territorial behaviors may include singing or calling, flight displays, and other aggressive postures or movements. Birds usually are most aggressive toward intruders of the same species, but sometimes they also keep other species off their turf. Burrowing Owls are small, but they will aggressively attack mammals of any size that trot within striking range of their burrows.

Most owls are territorial to some degree. Some defend the nest site along with a feeding territory around the nest; others, such as Burrowing Owls, defend only the nest site. Some species, such as Western Screech-Owls, defend a territory all year long; others, such as Northern Hawk Owls, are territorial only around the nest site and only during the breeding season. Among Snowy Owls, females defend territories in winter, when males wander and are not territorial.

The size of the territories varies considerably. Big owls tend to have big territories, whereas small owls tend to have small ones. A pair of Great Horned Owls may claim 5 to 10 square kilometers, but a single square kilometer is big enough for four or five pairs of nesting Elf Owls.

A few owls are not territorial. In places where there are plenty of prey and nest sites, Barn Owls live in very close proximity, in what might be called colonies. They hunt together over the same fields, and even roost in groups at night. In northern forests, when prey populations are at their peak and there's plenty of food for all, the local owl species become less territorial.

Migration

Most owls aren't big travelers. They spend pretty much their entire lives in pretty much the same place. A few owl species are true migrants that make regular trips twice a year, in spring and fall. They travel along predictable paths between the northern breeding areas, where they raise their young, and southern areas where they spend the winter.

Two migratory species are the Elf Owl and the Flammulated Owl. With these owls, it's a case of migrate or starve. Both are small, both are insect eaters, both forage exclusively at night—and in the northern parts of their ranges, there are no insects flying around on frosty winter nights. So they head south in fall. Elf Owls leave Arizona—the northernmost part of their range—and head for Mexico. Exactly where Flammulated Owls go is more complicated. These owls live on western mountain slopes in three nations, from Canada through the United States to Mexico. When fall rolls around, Flammulated Owls in southern Mexico are thought to stay put; meanwhile, all the others migrate south. The end result is that there are no Flammulated Owls in Canada and the United States in winter; instead, the entire population is in Mexico and Guatemala.

Flammulated Owls seem to move in a leisurely way on their fall travels, and they choose a course that keeps them at fairly high elevations. In the spring, however, they head north fast and stick to the lower slopes, where it's warmer and insects are more likely to be active.

The Northern Saw-whet Owl is another small owl that migrates, although not for lack of insect prey, as these owls eat mostly mice and voles. In the spring and summer, saw-whet owls breed in fingers of habitat stretching from southern Alaska along the Pacific coast to Southern California, south from British Columbia through the Rockies, and east from British Columbia across southern Canada and the United States. There are also disjunct populations in the mountains of central Mexico. In all of these areas, some saw-whet owls seem to stick around year-round, while others, mostly the youngest birds, migrate.

Until very recently, scientists knew almost nothing about saw-whet owl movements. In the 1990s, researchers in the Great Lakes, New England, and mid-Atlantic states got together to form Project Owlnet. Now, each fall, teams of researchers at a network of nature centers and research stations catch, band, and release migrating saw-whet owls. Preliminary results suggest that the Ohio River Valley, which follows the southern borders of Ohio, Indiana, and Illinois, is one important migration corridor, and that other owls follow the Atlantic coast corridor from Maine to North Carolina and traverse the central Appalachians in Pennsylvania. Like many songbirds, saw-whet owls migrate at night, when there are clear skies and northwest winds to help push them along.

Burrowing Owls, like Elf Owls and Flammulated Owls, are small and eat a lot of insects. As with Northern Saw-whets, only a subset of the population migrates. These long-legged, feisty owls can be found in the prairies of southern Canada and the United States, south into Mexico, and all the way down to

OWL BANDING

In 1803, while living on his family's estate in the Philadelphia suburbs, eighteen-year-old John James Audubon became fascinated by some phoebes nesting in the orchard. He wondered whether the same birds returned to the orchard each year. So when the nestful of eggs hatched, Audubon carefully tied silver threads around the legs of the chicks. Imagine his delight when the next spring, his marked phoebes returned as adults to the very same tree.

Audubon's exercise was one of the earliest examples of a now-common practice called bird banding. Banding usually involves crimping a thin, flexible metal band, imprinted with a unique identifying number, around a bird's ankle.

Before you can attach the band, you have to catch the bird. There are various ways to do this. Waterfowl researchers use cannons to launch nets over resting flocks; this is the most spectacular method. But by far the most common way to catch birds for banding is with a device called a mist net.

Once it's set up, a mist net looks a bit like a volleyball net—a long mesh panel hung from two poles. The net itself is made of very fine black nylon, and placed in a shadowy forest, it's all but invisible. Bird banders often use recorded calls to attract birds to the area. The birds fly into the mesh and get mildly tangled up. A researcher untangles the birds, weighs and measures them, squeezes on a band, and releases them.

Because the birds are assigned unique identifying numbers, if a bird is later recaptured, or if the band is recovered from a dead bird, scientists can learn quite a lot, including how long birds live and where they travel during their lifetime. By learning more about the paths owls and other birds follow on migration, scientists can help ensure that the habitat birds need to rest and refuel on their arduous journeys is protected.

South America, where they live everywhere except the Amazon basin. Burrowing Owls that breed in the northernmost part of their North American range—that is, in Canada and the northern United States—migrate south in winter to places like Oklahoma, Texas, southern Arizona, New Mexico, and northern Mexico. Burrowing Owls in the southern United States (including an isolated population in Florida) and those in Central and South America are year-round residents.

Some birds make what are called altitudinal migrations. These birds breed on mountain slopes at high elevations. When autumn comes, they don't fly south for the winter. They simply head downhill, because at lower elevations, conditions are better: winter temperatures are milder, snow doesn't pile as deep, there's protection from the wind. Some populations of Northern Pygmy-Owls, Northern Saw-whet Owls, and Northern Spotted Owls are thought to make regular altitudinal migrations.

Other owl species show irregular patterns of movement. Great Gray Owls, Boreal Owls, Snowy Owls, and Northern Hawk Owls are the species best known for this behavior. At three- to five-year intervals, a subset of the population may wander southward in winter, showing up far outside the species'

Many bird banders are not scientists, but amateurs—bird-watchers who enjoy seeing birds up close and making a contribution to scientific knowledge of bird migration and other mysteries. It does take special training to be a bander, however. (See the Resources section at the back of this book for more information.)

This Northern Saw-whet Owl will get a numbered leg band as part of a study of little owls' migration paths.

normal year-round range—to the delight of local bird-watchers. The Arctic-dwelling Snowy Owl has been sighted as far south as North Carolina, Utah, and California. In 2001, birders in southeastern Manitoba were thrilled to spot more than a hundred Great Gray Owls in a single day.

Scientists think food shortages may be the impetus for the southern invasions. Northern owl species all tend to be dietary specialists, relying mostly on just one or a few species of small rodents. Great Gray Owls favor meadow voles; Boreal Owls tend to take red-backed voles or pocket gophers; and Snowy Owls primarily feed on lemmings. All of these small rodent species undergo regular population cycles at three- to five-year intervals. When rodents are plentiful, owl populations increase. When rodent numbers drop, owls are forced to look elsewhere for food.

Food shortages don't tell the whole story, however, because even when it's not an "invasion year," at least some members of each population still wander south. Consider Snowy Owls: at least a few of the big white owls show up each winter at Boston's Logan Airport. Some evidence suggests that young of the year that can't find territories may be more likely to move along, but more research is needed.

3

Habits

Wrangel Island is in the middle of the Arctic Ocean, north of the Russian mainland. The Snowy Owls that winter here use an unusual hunting strategy. Oh, they scan the flat tundra landscape, all right, but not just for prey. They're also looking for a fellow hunter, the arctic fox.

As these white foxes trot energetically across the flat, windswept tundra, they pause now and then to cock their heads and listen—checking for lemmings, which, in winter, live in tunnels below the snow. If a fox hears squeaking or scurrying feet, it digs down through the snow or pounces to break through the surface.

If the fox emerges from the snow with a lemming in its jaws, the owl swings into action. It attacks the fox, talons-first. The startled fox may drop its meal to defend itself with snapping jaws. That's what the owl is waiting for. It takes quick evasive action, neatly grabs the lemming, and wings away.

Owls use several strategies to hunt their prey; this is just one of the more sensational ones. They also use different strategies to stay warm, keep in touch with each other, and evade those who hunt them.

Hunting Strategies

When it's time to find a meal, some animals have it easy. A groundhog in a meadow might as well be standing in a great big salad bowl. Oysters in shallow coastal waters simply open their shells to let ocean currents sweep the food particles right in. Making a living as a hunter is much harder. It takes skill.

As carnivores, owls are hunters. They have exceptional eyesight, keen ears, sharp powerful beaks, strong feet, and needle-sharp talons, and they use these tools to hunt in a variety of ways.

The hunting strategy that owls use most often is simply to sit and wait. The owl chooses an elevated perch near an open area. It sits quietly, watching and listening, until it either sees or hears a likely target. Then it orients its head and body so that it is facing its prey. It launches from the perch and usually flies straight at the target, although some owls approach their prey stealthily.

At the last minute, the owl raises its wings, swings its feet forward into the space occupied a moment earlier by its head, and closes its eyes to protect them. At the same time, its outside toes swing forward into the two-forward, two-back configuration, so that the owl hits its target with talons widespread. It may snatch up the unlucky mouse or vole, or pin it to the ground. The illustrations on the following pages show step by step how a Northern Saw-whet Owl takes an unsuspecting deer mouse.

An owl strikes fast and hard—sometimes hard enough to break a small animal's spine. It fixes its prey in a crushing grip, so that the needle-tipped talons drive deep into the soft body, puncturing vital internal organs. To give you a sense of how strong an owl's feet are, a Great Horned Owl can exert 500 pounds of pressure per square inch with just one foot. That's comparable to the force that a wolf exerts with its jaws.

In the unlikely event that the prey survives the strike, the owl kills it quickly with a nip from its beak to the head or neck. After all, mice, rats, and squirrels can squirm and fight back, and they have sharp teeth and claws of their own. A quick kill reduces the risk that the owl will be injured.

Prey subdued, the owl may stand over its prize for a few moments, with its wings and tail spread wide in a posture called mantling. (Hawks and eagles also mantle their prey.) This term comes from the word *mantle*, meaning a cloak, something you toss over your shoulders. An owl standing erect with its wings spread wide looks a bit like a person wearing a flowing cloak.

But standing still on the forest floor, an owl is vulnerable. The hunter is at risk of becoming the hunted. So after making the kill, an owl usually takes flight quickly, carrying its prey. Most birds use their beaks when they have to carry things. That's how the songbirds in your backyard carry sticks for a nest and ferry caterpillars to their offspring. Owls, along with hawks and eagles, are some of the few birds that carry prey in their feet.

If an owl is bringing food to the nest, it will transfer the catch from its talons to its beak before making the hand-off to the waiting female, which receives it with her beak. If a prey item is small, or if the owl has only a short distance to travel, it may choose to carry the prey home in its beak.

When they are hunting by the sit-and-wait method, most owls choose perches that are fairly low to the ground, for a good view, and they make fairly short flights to the target. Eastern Screech-Owls typically choose hunting perches about 6 to 10 feet up, on a horizontal branch. The Boreal Owl, another small species, tends to hunts from about 6 feet up.

One interesting study of Eastern Screech-Owls showed that they perch a little lower on dark nights and a little higher when the moon is full. Perhaps they perch higher on brighter nights for a wider field of view. Male and

A Northern Saw-whet Owl has spotted a deer mouse. It launches from its perch, eyes and ears pointed at the target. At the last moment, it swings its feet forward, lifts its wings to stall, then stretches its legs forward while spreading the talons wide, striking with their maximum surface area. Notice that the owl also closes its eyes, to protect them.

female Screech-Owls also station themselves differently when hunting: females tend to sit closer to the tree trunks, whereas males tend to go a little farther out on the limbs, perhaps because the males are smaller and lighter and don't need such a thick branch for support.

Although sit-and-wait hunting is the most common strategy for owls, it's hardly the only one. Another strategy is coursing—flying low and slow, in a

TOOL USE BY OWLS

Burrowing Owls have a funky habit. On their foraging trips over the prairie, they pick up bits of dung—cowpies, horse manure, dog dirt, whatever—and bring the stuff home to line their underground burrows. They also arrange the smelly treasures around the entrances to their burrows.

Scientists have wondered, and reasonably so: What's the purpose of this strange behavior? There's some evidence that a burrow lined with dung stays cooler than an unlined burrow during hot prairie summers. Another idea is that dung is a kind of smelly camouflage, keeping predators away by masking the smell of eggs and owlets inside the burrow.

Recently, however, a team of Florida researchers came up with a new explanation. According to University of Florida–Gainesville zoologist Douglas Levey and his team of student assistants, Burrowing Owls use dung as bait to "fish" for dung beetles. The beetles smell the bait and fly right to the owls' doorsteps—dinner that delivers itself.

The Florida researchers confirmed this idea with an experiment. They stripped a dozen burrows of dung, then replaced the dung at half the burrows, leaving the other half dung-free as controls. At the end of four days, the researchers collected all the pellets the owls had coughed up after eating and checked them for the remains of prey. Owls living in the dung-lined burrows ate ten times as many dung beetles, and six times as many kinds of dung beetle, as owls in dung-free burrows.

It makes sense that a fresh pile of dung would lure beetles. Dung beetles routinely smell their way to food. On warm days, they make low, coursing flights, checking for the scent of their next meal.

The Florida researchers say that in bringing dung to their burrows, these owls are using a tool to catch their food. Other examples of tool use by birds include Woodpecker Finches on the Galápagos Islands that use cactus spines to dig for beetle grubs; Egyptian Vultures that toss stones at ostrich eggs to crack them open; and Green Herons that use "fishing lures," dropping bits of sticks or feathers on the water's surface, then spearing the minnows that rise to the bait. There's no systematic evidence that these birds eat better thanks to their tools, however. The Florida study is significant because it shows that owls that put dung around their burrows end up eating more beetles than owls that have no dung.

What about the idea that the odor of dung serves as a kind of olfactory camouflage for owl eggs? The Florida researchers tested this idea by digging experimental burrows and placing quail eggs inside. They lined some of the burrows with dung and left the others unlined. Predators quickly found and ate the eggs in both kinds of burrows.

zigzag pattern, across an open field or meadow. The graceful hawk called the Northern Harrier is best known for this hunting style, but Short-eared and Long-eared Owls—which, like the harrier, have long wings and light bodies— also hunt by coursing. So do Barn Owls.

A coursing owl flies very low, indeed—at an elevation of less than 10 feet. Sometimes it flaps its wings, sometimes it glides. As it flies, the owl looks straight down, directing its round facial disk at the ground so it can both watch and listen for mice or voles in the grass. A coursing owl may hover for a while, getting a bead on its target before dropping feet-first. At times, it may fly into the wind so that air currents loft it upward as much as 100 feet.

There are other ways to hunt on the wing. Many insect-eating birds use a strategy called fly catching, also known as hawking. They perch on a horizontal branch or a snag near an open area and scan the scene, then fly out from the perch to grab prey in midair. Maybe you've seen phoebes or kingbirds hawking after insects in a meadow or by a lake. Some owls also hunt this way. The small insect-eating species, such as Flammulated Owls and Elf Owls, often hawk after large moths. In contrast to songbirds, which catch prey in their beaks, an owl makes the grab in midair with its talons. It then transfers the catch to its beak in flight so it can land on a perch and eat.

Snowy Owls sometimes take prey on the wing, but you wouldn't exactly call their behavior fly catching. Large, fast, and powerful, a Snowy Owl can pursue and overtake a duck in flight. Usually, though, Snowies conserve their energy; if they're in the mood for duck, they'll take ducklings from the nest or swoop down on sick or wounded waterfowl. Snowies have even been known to hang around duck blinds and take wounded birds the hunters shoot down.

In addition to hawking, Flammulated Owls will "hover-glean," beating their wings like oversize hummingbirds so they can stay suspended in place while delicately picking insects from forest foliage.

Though owls are famous for the way their silent flight helps them get the drop on prey, a few species sometimes hunt without flying at all. They use a strategy called ground stalking. Burrowing owls do this routinely. These prairie dwellers eat lots of beetles in summer, and they chase them down on foot.

Other owls ground-stalk occasionally. A Great Horned Owl that sees a rabbit or mouse disappear into a thicket or dense grass may land on the ground and stride deliberately after the escapee. Barred Owls, which tend to live near swamps, wade into the water after small fish and crayfish, which they catch with their feet. Snowy Owls also wade after small fish and crustaceans in tundra ponds or tide pools.

Eating Habits

A Barn Owl has captured a field mouse. It returns to the safety of its perch in the rafters of an abandoned barn. Now what? The owl holds the mouse in its beak, gives a little toss of its head to align the body, and swallows its meal. As

Above: *A Great Gray Owl plunges straight at the snow-covered ground. It can hear a vole, hidden in a tunnel beneath the snow.* Right: *After making the kill, the owl looks around, to make sure no foxes lurk nearby. Then it takes flight with its prize.*

SNOW PLUNGING

A logging road winds through a forest in western Canada. At the road's edge, a Great Gray Owl sits motionless in a tree. It seems to be doing typical sit-and-wait hunting, for it is staring intently downward. To the casual observer, though, this behavior seems a little odd, because there's nothing of obvious interest below. The forest floor is a featureless blanket of crusted and glittering snow.

Suddenly the big owl launches from its perch, folds its wings, and plunges headfirst like a cliff diver in Acapulco. It's a breathtaking moment. The big bird seems to be committing suicide.

Just when it seems the owl will crash and break its neck, it lifts its wings slightly to break its fall and swings its legs forward so that it plunges through the snow feetfirst. It may disappear from sight in the snow, but only for a moment. Quickly the round gray dome of its head pokes up over the rim of the snow hole. The owl looks around. It clambers upward, spreads its wings, and takes flight—with a vole clutched in its talons.

How did the owl know it would find the little rodent in that exact spot? Great Gray Owls do have excellent vision, but they can't see through snow. They use their keen sense of hearing to locate prey. They can detect faint squeaks and the sounds of scurrying footsteps through as much as 2 feet of snow, while perched in a tree branch as far as 30 yards away from the source of the sound.

Great Grays are also powerful enough to punch their feet through an ice crust half an inch thick and capable of supporting the weight of a large human being. With their long legs, these owls can reach deep into the snow to make the grab.

Among the North American owls, Great Grays are definitely the snow-plunging champions, using this hunting strategy routinely. Other species, including Barred Owls, Boreal Owls, and Northern Hawk Owls, snow-plunge occasionally, but these smaller species can't break through icy snow crusts. That's why they tend to hunt in deep woods, where conifer trees shade the snow surface, preventing it from crusting.

long as the prey is small enough, that's the owl routine—just swallow it head-first. No ceremony, no dainty small bites.

Wolfing down meals makes sense for an owl. If it took the time to fussily dissect its prey, it could be vulnerable to attack from a predator. Also, certain birds, including ravens and eagles, are known to steal from owls, so that's

SNAKES IN THE NEST

A Texas researcher studying nesting Eastern Screech-Owls discovered something strange in their nests: One out of every five nests had an extra occupant—a live snake. These weren't big rat snakes, the kind that slither in to eat the owl eggs. They were tiny snakes, about the size and color of a large earthworm—far too small to eat an owl's eggs. They were *Leptotyphlops dulcis*, Texas blind snakes.

Blind snakes are related to boa constrictors, but they are much smaller. Several species of blind snakes live in North America. Some are truly eyeless and blind; others, including the Texas snake, have vestigial eyes hidden under scales; and a few actually have functional eyes.

Texas blind snakes ordinarily live in stony desert habitat, but they also show up in suburban gardens and around house foundations. They hunker under logs or rocks by day, coming out at night to feed on earthworms, ants, and termites.

That's when the screech-owls pick them up. But though owls are expert predators, they often carry blind snakes back to the nest alive. Perhaps owls choose to do this, or perhaps it's because blind snakes fight back when attacked, simultaneously defecating and releasing a noxious, smelly liquid, then writhing so that the slippery mess coats their smooth bodies. (Ordinarily, the snakes use this chemical defense to repel termites and ants as they raid their nests to feast on eggs and young.)

Owls seem to end up dropping off live snakes in their nests pretty often—and that's where things get interesting. You'd think a burrow-dwelling snake stranded in a tree would be the proverbial fish out of water, but actually, the bottom of an owl's nest makes a nice home. It's a messy mulch of owl feces, coughed-up owl pellets, and the remains of prey such as mice and beetles. Over time, the food and debris start to rot and get infested with insects—perfect for the blind snake, which tunnels right in and gets to work, gobbling up ants and fly maggots.

Research has shown that owlets in nests with resident blind snakes grow faster and are ready to leave the nest sooner than owlets in snake-free nests. Scientists aren't sure why. Some evidence suggests that thanks to the snakes' cleanup service, the food stored in the nest may last longer, which may mean more calories for the young owls. Another idea is that the young owls stay healthier in a pest-free nest.

Do owls choose to put snakes in their nests because they're beneficial? No one knows. It's possible that owls provision their nests with live snakes because they don't decay the way dead mice and beetles do. They stay nice and fresh, and they may even grow and fatten if well fed. Perhaps bringing home live snakes is just another way to keep the owl larder well stocked. Careful examination of owl pellets shows that the screech-owls do sometimes kill and eat these snakes.

another risk—losing a meal to a thief. Rough table manners also make sense for owlets, even though they are eating in the protection of their tree-hole nest. Siblings compete for food, so swallowing fast is the best way to be sure to get one's share.

Eating fast and swallowing prey is not entirely without risks. One observer reported that an Eastern Screech-Owl chick, trying to gulp down an entire nuthatch, died when, in the struggle to swallow, the songbird's bill punctured the roof of its mouth and penetrated its brain.

Owls can swallow pretty big items for their size. But what if the prey is more than one mouthful? Northern Pygmy-Owls, which are not much bigger than a large sparrow, sometimes take quail twice their size. Great Horned Owls can kill Canada Geese and house cats. Eating their prey whole isn't feasible in these situations, so owls break down their food into more manageable mouthfuls. Typically, an owl holds its prey down with one foot or just stands right on top, and uses its beak to tear the body apart. Owls are neat in their butchering, leaving behind an intact skeleton well stripped of flesh.

Sometimes small prey needs processing too. Eastern Screech-Owls pluck and discard crayfish's sharp claws before swallowing the rest. Owls that catch small birds pluck off some of the indigestible feathers. And sometimes, owls that aren't too hungry get picky about their snacks. When lemmings are plentiful, Snowy Owls may catch one after another but eat only the heads, the most energy-packed part. After a meal, these white owls wipe their faces in the snow or grass to clean the blood from their feathers.

Caching

Most birds have a crop, a pouch inside the throat. This anatomical feature is a kind of built-in tote bag, useful for storing extra food. If a bird happens across a food bonanza, it can eat its fill, then pack more food in the crop. Later on, once there's room in its digestive tract, the bird can finish swallowing what's in the crop, or it may carry the food home, then neatly cough up dinner for its nestlings.

Owls don't have crops, but they have no trouble carrying food home to their young with their powerful feet. To put away extra food for later consumption, owls often cache food: if they kill extra prey, they simply tuck it away in a safe place to eat later.

A Northern Spotted Owl that has eaten its fill and spots yet another flying squirrel may go ahead and make the kill, then cram the body in a safe place, such as the crotch of a tree. Later the next morning, if it feels hungry, it will rouse from its roost and retrieve the snack. A father screech-owl that is hunting to feed his family caches food in a slightly different way: he brings the extra food home to the nest hole, where the mother owl stacks it up inside like cordwood, ready to be served as the owlets demand.

A number of birds are known for their caching habits: Acorn Woodpeckers store acorns, for example, and Clark's Nutcrackers hide pine seeds. Seeds are relatively nonperishable, and these birds may leave them cached for weeks to months. In winter, when there's natural refrigeration, owls may also leave cached prey undisturbed for long periods. But carcasses don't stay fresh for long in warm weather, so owls retrieve food from caches after hours to days, then replace it with fresh prey if they can.

Caching is an especially handy trait for small owls with high metabolic rates that need frequent meals. The pygmy-owls are known for their caching behavior, and Elf Owls often cram extra snakes, lizards, or mice in their nest holes. Caching probably helps Eastern Screech-Owls survive northern winters. The Northern Saw-whet Owl is another species known for piling up food when temperatures are dropping.

In winter, though stored food stays fresh, those dead mice, voles, and rats may become frozen solid. Owls simply sit on the frozen food until it thaws, which takes about half an hour. This behavior is not so different from what a female owl does when she incubates her eggs—though it must be a lot less comfortable.

Digestion

Say a Barn Owl has swallowed a rat—fur, whiskers, scaly tail, and all. The rat slides headfirst down the owl's esophagus and then through the proventriculus, the glandular part of the stomach, where it gets coated with digestive juices. It lodges in the gizzard, the muscular part of the stomach, which starts contracting and churning. The gizzard does the work of teeth, chewing up the food, while the stomach juices (a mixture of digestive enzymes, hydrochloric acid, and mucus) go to work on the soft tissues, breaking them down so that nutrients can be absorbed and distributed throughout the owl's body.

Owls have fairly weak digestive juices in contrast to hawks and eagles, which also swallow their prey whole or in big chunks. These birds have powerful stomach juices, up to six times as acidic as an owl's. Most birds of prey, or raptors, can digest a fair amount of bone, fur, and feathers, although they usually end up with some leftovers. But after an owl's stomach churns the good stuff off the bones, there's quite a ball of indigestible bits left in the gizzard.

If this prickly mass were allowed to pass from the gizzard into the intestine, it could interfere with the uptake of nutrients, and the sharp bones could pierce and tear the intestine, which could be deadly. Even if the bolus made it all the way through the intestine without problems, the bulky mass could end up obstructing the bird's cloaca (the common opening for the digestive, reproductive, and urinary tracts), possibly with a deadly outcome.

So owls get rid of the gunk another way. The powerful muscles of the gizzard compact the leftovers into a small, cylindrical pellet, tapered at both ends. When the time is right, the owl casts, or regurgitates, the pellet.

Owls produce pellets on a fairly regular cycle. In the course of a night's hunting, an owl may catch and swallow several prey items; their remains get compressed together into a single pellet. The pellet can remain lodged in the

An owl pellet contains the indigestible parts of an owl's meal, such as bones, fur, and feathers. By examining these remains, scientists can tell what the owl has been eating.

proventriculus for quite a while (some estimates say ten to twenty hours), but while the pellet is sitting there, the owl can't eat anything new—the pellet is in the way. So usually, after spending the day resting and digesting, the owl rouses itself, casts its pellet, and is ready to eat again.

If you happen to be around at the right time, you can see signs that an owl is ready to cast a pellet. It closes its eyes, and its facial disk seems to narrow. Observers say it looks almost as if the owl is in pain. Muscular contractions then send the pellet up the esophagus. The owl stretches its neck, leans forward facedown, opens its beak . . . and lets the pellet fall to the ground. Although this is often referred to as "coughing up" a pellet, the owl doesn't make any violent movements that resemble coughing or retching. Throwing up repeatedly can cause damage to the human esophagus from the repeated exposure to stomach acids, but owls' throats are protected by a thick coating of nonacidic mucus on the pellets.

An owl often has a favorite perch where it rests for most of the day, and it will cast a pellet from this perch before taking off to hunt at night. So a pile of pellets at the base of a tree is a sign that an owl's daily roost site is up above. It's also a clue to what species roosted there, because the size of the pellet is proportional to the size of the owl: up to 1 inch long for small species such as Northern Pygmy-Owls, and as much as 3 or 4 inches long for Great Horned Owls.

Avoiding Enemies

A Northern Saw-whet Owl is caught in a mist net at a banding station in Pennsylvania. As the bander tries to extricate the owl, it hisses and snaps its beak furiously, trying to bite. Saw-whets are quite fierce, but they're mighty mites, small enough to fit in the palm of your hand. So, even though these owls are formidable predators, they can themselves become prey. Last year, a Barred Owl haunted this banding station, picking off the little owls one by one as the banders released them.

Many kinds of hawks, eagles, and falcons will attack an owl. Peregrine Falcons have been known to take screech-owls. Great Gray Owls, the largest owls in North America, are targeted by Bald Eagles. And big owls prey on smaller

Long-eared Owls take "concealing posture" to the extreme. They compress their bodies until they appear almost impossibly slim.

ones. When their usual prey is scarce, Great Horned Owls attack Barred Owls and screech-owls.

Owls are vulnerable to predators when they are on the ground feeding and when they roost by day. Their first line of defense is their camouflage plumage, which helps them hide in plain sight while they sleep. Many owls also choose roost sites that are in very dense vegetation, such as in an evergreen tree, with its concealing foliage. Eastern Screech-Owls prefer a tree-hole roost.

A perched owl that perceives danger adopts what's called a concealing posture. It's a bit like what happens when a mother pokes a teenager in the back and says, "Stand up straight." The owl pulls itself up and stands very erect. Its body seems to squeeze together and compress so that it looks taller and thinner. If it has ear tufts, the owl erects them as well. With these adjustments to its posture, the owl looks like the broken stub of a tree branch. To improve the camouflage effect, owls that have white "eyebrow" feathers on their facial disks can fluff and rearrange these feathers so that they're somewhat concealed behind duller feathers. The image on the previous page shows a Long-eared Owl in a concealing posture.

An owl that is trying to conceal itself can adjust its posture in other ways. If it has been perching toward the middle of a tree branch, it shuffles sideways to press up against the tree trunk so that its feathers blend with the background of bark. It may also squeeze its eyes shut to conceal the bright yellow ring of the iris. An owl with white underparts may conceal them by folding one wing sideways across the chest, almost like Count Dracula in a movie, lifting his arm and bending his elbow to peer over his cape. And an owl that has rictal bristles, specialized feathers around the mouth, will push them forward to hide its beak.

Self-Defense

What if hiding in plain sight doesn't work? Or what if an owl is suddenly confronted by an enemy—say a farmer goes up to the loft and comes face-to-face with a Barn Owl, or an arctic fox attacks a female Snowy Owl on her nest? The owl shifts gears in a hurry, switching from slim and inconspicuous to large and menacing.

The owl's first response is to erect all its feathers, like a cat or dog raising its hackles. If its sudden increase in size isn't enough to make the intruder back off, the owl gets pugnacious. Like a fighter, it lowers its head while keeping its eyes locked on the attacker. It spreads its wings and tail wide, tilting the wings so that their widest surface faces the attacker. In this posture, the owl presents the maximum surface area to the intruder, making itself look as big as possible. The female Snowy Owl on page 46 is defending her nest.

To make its defensive display even scarier, the owl may hiss and clatter its beak. Barn Owls really go crazy, swaying back and forth and shaking their heads while hissing, snapping, and bowing.

The last line of defense is to fly away. But before doing so, Barn Owls have one other trick: they may fall down and play dead.

This Eastern Screech-Owl has been disturbed on its daytime roost, so it adjusts its body into a concealing pose. Its eyes close to slits, concealing the yellow irises. It also stands tall and lifts its ear tufts—the better to resemble a broken branch. Meanwhile, the owl sidles closer to the tree trunk, where its feathers will blend with the bark in the background.

MOBBING

The Great Horned Owl was sitting quietly in a golf course pine tree when the flock of crows arrived. The big black birds filled the air around the owl with sound and fury. After enduring the assault for a few minutes, the owl spread its wings and took flight. It headed for the shelter of a nearby woods, with the crows trailing after it like a pack of angry dogs.

Songbirds recognize that an owl is a predator—a danger to themselves and their nestlings. So when birds spot an owl, the flock may attack en masse, in a behavior called mobbing.

The precise reaction to an owl depends on the species. Some birds may just fly close; others fly close and call loudly; still others actually attack, trying to strike the owl's head or body with their claws. Crows, jays, mockingbirds, warblers, and chickadees are among the birds that often mob owls.

Superficially, mobbing behavior makes sense. Most owls prey on the occasional songbird, and some, including screech-owls, pygmy-owls, and Short-eared Owls, take quite a few birds. On the surface, mobbing seems to be a way for many little Davids to unite against a Goliath. A mob can force a potentially dangerous predator to move out of the neighborhood.

Those who have studied mobbing behavior, however, say this explanation may be too simplistic. Not all owls targeted by songbird mobs seem upset or bothered by the experience. Owls usually move on—but they may stay put. Also, owls are rarely injured by a mob. The smaller birds may get close enough to pull on the owl's feathers, but they usually don't cause any harm.

Another consideration is that the daytime attacks by mobs seem a little pointless. By day, an owl is not usually an immediate threat to songbirds. It is not hunting; it is trying to rest and digest its meal. Indeed, the owl probably couldn't catch one of the alert, attacking birds if it tried. Owls rely on the element of surprise to make their kills.

By their willingness to attack noisily, songbirds may be indicating that they know they are not in any real danger. When these little birds spot a bird-eating predator that is ordinarily active by day, such as a Peregrine Falcon, they react very differently: They find cover, freeze, and use very soft alarm calls (not loud squawks) to announce the danger to other birds in the flock so that the predator won't notice them.

Finally, mobbing behavior is more common in spring and summer, when songbirds are raising chicks, than in fall, when migratory songbirds begin their long journeys. Thus it's possible that mobbing is a kind of self-defense class for young birds—that by example, parents are teaching young birds how to recognize a threat.

Although owls are usually the target of mobs, some owls do a little mobbing of their own. Short-eared Owls often attack larger predatory birds, such as eagles and hawks. It may be that the owls are defending their turf—they don't want the bigger birds poaching their prospective prey. But some observers say that the owls just seem to be having a good time.

Regulating Body Temperature

From the Arctic in winter to the Sonoran Desert in summer, owls can be found a range of extreme environments in North America. They keep warm or cool in a variety of ways.

Because they are warm-blooded animals, owls must keep their metabolic furnaces stoked with plenty of food. One reason they are so successful in cold climates is because of their hunting skill: they can keep themselves supplied with a steady stream of calorie-dense food. Owls also convert extra calories to reserves of energy-rich fat. These factors, along with their habit of caching food, keep them well fed during temporary lean times.

If making themselves look slim and inconspicuous doesn't work, owls will go on the defensive. To repel a fox that is trying to steal her eggs, this female Snowy Owl makes herself look as big and scary as possible. She also snaps her beak and hisses.

Many owls keep warm while they sleep by roosting in tree holes or in evergreen trees with dense foliage. These enclosed retreats not only foil predators, but also keep owls warmer than exposed sleep sites.

Feathers obviously keep owls warm. If you've ever snuggled under a down comforter, you know that feathers can keep you very warm while adding very little weight. Their loose, springy structure creates spaces where warm air is trapped. Many birds have a layer of down underneath their smooth, outer contour feathers; the down is what keeps them warm. Owls, however, have only a few of these specialized down feathers; instead, most of their contour features are dual-purpose, with a downy area near the base and a smooth area at the top. But that's enough to do the job.

Most birds have bare, unfeathered feet, but the northern-dwelling owls have feathered legs and toes. These feathers may help keep the extremities warm, though it's also possible that countercurrent exchange in the blood vessels of the legs is sufficient to maintain the feet's temperature, and that the toe feathers serve mainly to protect an owl's feet from lively prey that tries to bite back.

Owls that live in northern forests face an interesting thermoregulation challenge: the feathers that keep them so warm in subzero winters can be too warm in midsummer, when temperatures push up into the 70s or 80s. Some owls seek out sheltered roost spots in winter, places that are warmer on average than the rest of the forest. But Boreal Owls have such warm feathers that they don't need to do this. Boreal Owls face a different challenge: They risk overheating in summer. So they seek out the coolest, shadiest roosting spots—locations that are measurably cooler than the average forest location.

All owls keep cool on really hot days by panting like dogs and by drooping their wings so that air can circulate to the featherless areas beneath. Burrowing Owls, which live in wide open spaces, escape summer heat in their underground retreats.

Owls that are active at night rest by day—a behavior that is called roosting. This Barred Owl has chosen a safe and secluded roost site inside a hollow tree.

Preening

When we say a person is preening, we mean they're acting vain or primping in front of a mirror. When birds preen, however, it's not a sign of vanity—it's a matter of life and death.

Feathers are essential. Without a working set of feathers, a bird can't fly. It can't find food, escape enemies, or stay warm and dry. Preening keeps feathers in good condition. No wonder owls, like all birds, spend hours each day preening.

Two main activities are involved in preening: a simple stroking motion of the beak, to smooth the feather surfaces, and a nibbling action, where the bird moves its beak along the length of each feather from the base to the tip. Birds may also preen with a firmer, swifter action, gripping the feather with the beak, then sliding the beak the length of the feather from base to tip, like a beautician pulling a hank of hair through her fingers.

Preening is good for feathers in several ways. For one thing, it puts disarranged feathers back in their proper places and configurations. Feathers are made up of thousands of smaller strands that hook together with tiny barbs. If the strands get unhooked during the day's activities, preening zips them back together. Owls that are preening often shake and stretch their wings, which also helps arrange the feathers.

The stroking and nibbling also gets feathers clean, removing dust and debris, as well as blood or slime from the latest meal. And preening gets rid of itchy and debilitating parasites such as lice.

It even helps keep feathers waterproof. While preening, the owl turns its head from time to time and presses its beak against its uropygial gland, located above the base of its tail. The gland releases oil, which the owl spreads over its feathers with its beak. A fresh coating of oil causes rainwater to bead up and run off the feathers. Preen oil also contains antibacterial and antifungal agents.

Oiling the feathers brings one other benefit. Ultraviolet light converts compounds in the preen oil to vitamin D. Then, the next time the owl preens, it takes in a healthy dose of this important vitamin, which the body needs to process calcium. Though they are creatures of the night, owls do like to sunbathe, if they can do so safely. An owl resting on its daytime perch adjusts its position like a beachgoer dragging a lounge chair around, moving with the sun to catch the best rays. When it's got just the right position, it relaxes, lolling with its mouth open and its eyes closed.

Owls may preen with their talons as well as their beaks. In fact, the Barn Owl has a special comblike structure on the middle talon that is used just for preening. Because an owl can't preen its own head with its beak, it uses its talons to groom this area, or it may solicit help from another owl.

Mutual preening is a very common owl activity. The behavior seems to make owls less aggressive toward one another. Courting owls strengthen their pair-bond by preening each other. Parents and their chicks also engage in mutual preening. One scientist who has banded many Great Gray Owls and

Northern Hawk Owls reports that if you bend your head down to an owl, it will preen your hair for you. (The bent head is a posture of submission that owls take as an invitation to preen.) This trick doesn't work if you are bald, however.

Vocalizations

Owls communicate with one another through vocalizations. Ask a toddler what the owl says, and she'll answer, *"Hoo-hoo."* Many owls do make low-pitched sounds that sound to human ears like hooting; this is why some people call Great Horned Owls and Barred Owls "hoot-owls." Not all owls hoot, however. And the owls that do hoot also make quite a variety of other sounds. Night-flying owl species have the biggest repertoires; day-active owls are less talkative.

The Barn Owl is one species that never hoots. This owl is best known for its blood-chilling screech, a sound that it often lets loose while flying. Despite deficiencies in the hooting department, Barn Owls have quite an extensive vocal repertoire: They also make purring sounds and a noise that sounds remarkably like snoring; chirrup and twitter to one another; and snap their bills and hiss at intruders.

As this list suggests, owls use different calls to exchange different kinds of information. At the start of the breeding season, owls call to establish and defend a territory and to locate and attract a mate. A Flammulated Owl proclaims, "Hey, I'm here, on my territory," by giving a low, repeated hoot, often transcribed as *boop.* He repeats this call monotonously, every two to four seconds. If another male intrudes on his turf, he says, "Back off!" with a speeded-up, three-syllable *boop-boop-boop.* Similarly, the Eastern Screech-Owl gives its familiar "whinny" call, which sounds like a neighing horse, to warn off intruding males. The male Barn Owl's distinctive scream announces, "This is my territory!" and at the same time gets the attention of any unattached female within earshot, which may scream back.

During courtship rituals, a male and female usually exchange softer notes, sometimes described as chuckling sounds. Once a male and female owl pair up, they "talk" back and forth to reinforce their relationship. You may hear members of an owl pair calling back and forth to one another on the territory; both Great Horned Owl and Barred Owl pairs often do this, in their familiar hooting voices.

Owl parents also "talk" to their chicks. When the male brings food to the nest, the members of the family twitter back and forth. Female Barn Owls let their mates know they are hungry with an unusual call that sounds like snoring. Chicks beg for food from their parents and quarrel with their nestmates. And when Great Horned Owl chicks make their first flights, parents use a whistled call to keep in touch.

Finally, owls vocalize in the face of danger or to warn other owls. The alarm call of a Flammulated Owl sounds like a barking dog. When facing down an intruder, in addition to adopting the threat posture, owls attempt to appear more menacing by hissing and snapping their bills loudly. Parents that hear their chicks snapping their bills will fly in to defend them.

4

The Yearly Cycle

It's early January in a New England forest. Each tree branch is edged with snow like neatly piped white icing. More snow covers the forest floor in a thick, insulating blanket. According to the calendar, winter has just begun. Yet there's one clear sign that spring is on the way: the sound of a bird's voice breaking the stillness of the frozen, moonlit night.

This is not the chorus of birdsong we usually associate with spring. It's not the cheery lilt of a robin or wren, or the sunny *conk-a-ree* of a Red-winged Blackbird. No, this is a deep, hollow, hooting sound—the voice of a male Great Horned Owl calling for a mate.

Finding a Mate

When it comes to mating, owls are the proverbial early birds. Of all the birds that breed in North America, they are among the first to start looking for mates. Great Horned Owls may begin their hooting love duets in late December, and they may be sitting on eggs by late January or early February, while the snow is still thick on the ground.

Each owl species launches its breeding effort at a slightly different time, and the timing of breeding depends in part on each species' feeding habits. Great Horned Owls can get started early with their breeding efforts because they are generalists that take many kinds of prey; even in winter, they have no problem finding enough food to feed a brood. Owls that eat a lot of insects don't breed so early; they wait until warmer weather, when insects are more active and plentiful.

When owls start breeding also depends on location. Owls living at warmer southern latitudes start to breed sooner than owls of the same species living at colder northern latitudes.

Owls are not what you'd call sociable creatures. Most species don't gather in foraging flocks to hunt for food in the winter, the way other forest birds such as Common Redpolls, Pygmy Nuthatches, and turkeys do. And most owls don't gather in groups to roost at night, the way crows and grackles do.

Long-eared and Short-eared Owls are two notable exceptions. Both species are migratory, and while they are on their southern wintering grounds, they often hunt and roost in groups. The Barn Owl is another species that hunts over open grasslands and can be rather sociable. Barn Owls that raise their young in northern areas may also move south for the winter, and during their trips south, they sometimes roost in groups of as many as fifty.

But most owls are solitary souls and make their own way in the forest. A pair of owls, one male and one female, may share a territory all year long, but most of the time they don't do a lot of socializing.

A male Barred Owl (left) offers his significantly larger mate a gift of food. This behavior, called "courtship feeding," is common among owls. The female will rely on the male to continue feeding her while she sits on the eggs.

When mating season rolls around, though, loner owls get the urge to merge. Their behavior changes in response to a change in the amount of daylight to which they are exposed. After the winter solstice, days slowly become longer. There's a little bit more sunlight in each twenty-four-hour period. Sunlight striking the eyes sends a message to the owl's pituitary gland, the so-called "master gland" located at the base of the brain. This gland causes hormones to be released, and they circulate in the owl's blood.

Pituitary hormones act on the sex organs. The male's testes, the organs that produce sperm, grow larger, as does the female's ovary, the structure that makes eggs. (Human females usually have two active ovaries, but birds have just one active.) The hormones also spur owls to a variety of courtship behaviors.

Courtship Behaviors

The first order of business is to either locate a new mate or spruce up the relationship with an old mate through courtship behaviors. Bird courtship behavior usually includes some common elements that you may have seen right in your backyard. In a typical courtship sequence, the male bird sings loudly from a perch in his territory. He chases away other males if they try to enter his turf—and initially, he also chases away females.

Then his aggression toward females turns to interest. He lets them approach. He may show off in some way, by vocalizing, fanning his tail, bowing, flying around in an elaborate pattern, or all of the above. He may offer a female a morsel of food. And he may try to lead her to a lovely nest site. A singing warbler is advertising his availability; a male cardinal sitting by the feeder, offering seeds to a female, is engaging in courtship feeding; and a male House Wren hustling around the yard building several nests is also courting.

Not much is known about owl courtship, because not many scientists have studied it. With night-active owls, it's probably due to the logistical challenge of doing research at night. Or perhaps scientists haven't studied owl courtship because many North American owls live in cold, inaccessible places far from human habitation, and begin their courtship rituals while the land is still in the grip of winter. But a few studies have shed some light on the moonlit romance of owls.

If you were to deliberately listen for owls every night of the year, you'd notice that most species are most talkative in winter to early spring. This increase in vocalization signals the very beginning of courtship. (Owls can also be talkative in early fall, when they are establishing their territories for the winter.)

Even in species where the male and female stay together all year long, the pair become more talkative at the beginning of breeding season. Scientists think this chatty behavior helps strengthen the pair bond. The pair may become more attentive to each other in other ways, such as by perching close together.

At the very beginning of the breeding season, a male may chase away any owl, male or female, that gets close to the nesting site. Then subtly, this behavior changes. When he chases after a female, it's a less aggressive act, more like teenagers playing tag on the beach.

Long-eared and Short-eared Owl males embark on show-offy display flights for the females, clapping their wings loudly as they go. The male Barn Owl makes several kinds of display flights: song flights, during which he screeches in midair; moth flights, in which he hovers in midair before a female; and in-and-out flights, where he flies in and out of the nest site like an oversize bluebird, as if to show the female what a great piece of real estate he has claimed.

Mutual preening is an affectionate-looking way for owls to cement their relationship. Ritual feeding is another important part of the courtship process for owls, and this behavior is common to many species. The male goes hunting and brings back some item of prey, which he holds in his beak. He perches next to the female and offers her the token. Studies show that gifts of extra food are more than just a gesture for Barn Owls; the extra calories may help the female bulk up for the energy-demanding job of egg laying that lies ahead.

It's not clear if a female owl judges whether her mate will be a good provider by the gifts he brings her. But his willingness to provide food for her—and her willingness to accept it—will be important in the weeks ahead, because the female will rely on the male to feed her as she lays eggs, incubates them, and then broods the young owlets.

Mating

Copulation or mating, which ornithologists call treading, takes place after the buildup of courtship. In Great Horned Owls, the act follows a passionate, hooted duet; in Barn Owls, a gift of food is the prelude. Typically, the female gives a soft call and crouches down, and the male steps up on her back. He

keeps his balance by spreading his‚wings wide or flapping them and by seiz-
ing the nape of her neck in his beak. Afterward, he may sleep while she preens
him, or in some species, the pairs fly to separate trees and that's it.

Most owls are thought to be monogamous, meaning that the male and
female don't take other partners. In recent years, however, thanks to the
development of DNA paternity tests, scientists have discovered that many
birds thought to be strictly monogamous actually engage in extrapair copulations, mating with birds other than their partners. Researchers learned this by
drawing tiny blood samples from chicks in nests; the lab test can reveal
whether all chicks have the same father. As far as scientists know, only Burrowing Owls and Flammulated Owls indulge in extrapair copulations. That
doesn't necessarily mean that this behavior is absent in other owls—it's just
that so far, no one has really looked for it.

Nesting

Many songbirds build elaborate, cup-shaped nests from materials such as
grass, sticks, moss, and mud. Owls don't go in for fancy nest construction.
They just find a good place and claim it for their own.

What's a good place? Most owls prefer enclosed spaces, such as a hole in a
tree or a cliffside cave. The smallest owls, including Boreal Owls, Elf Owls,
Flammulated Owls, and Northern Saw-whet Owls, often nest in holes that
woodpeckers have pecked out, nested in, then abandoned. Large owls need a
larger space, such as a hollow tree. Great Gray Owls sometimes nest in snags,
dead trees with the tops snapped off. As the trunk starts to rot, a sunken hollow forms at the top. It's open to the sky but still offers some concealment.

Many of the owls that nest in tree holes will also use nest boxes, large
wooden birdhouses. Eastern and Western Screech-Owls, which find suburban
backyards to be acceptable habitat, take to nest boxes just fine. Grape growers in
California put up boxes for Barn Owls around their orchards, and then enjoy the
natural pest control the owls provide by hunting rats and mice. In some western
states and Canada, researchers put out nest boxes for Boreal Owls, encouraging
them to nest in known locations to make it easier to study populations.

Some owls that like to nest in caves and holes will also nest in buildings, as
long as they are dark and quiet. Barn Owls are named for their habit of nesting in barns, but they also routinely nest in silos and other farm outbuildings,
church steeples, attics, mine shafts, and under bridges.

Some owls don't require a completely enclosed space and will accept a
platform nest, basically a flat surface on which to lay eggs. Crows and hawks
build large nests out of sturdy sticks, use them for a season, and abandon
them . . . and then the next spring, the owls move in. Owls have even been
seen nesting atop clumps of mistletoe and abandoned squirrel nests.

In general, owls make no attempt to modify their nest sites. They don't add
a cozy, soft lining. Females may scrape a bit at the bottom of the nest, possibly
to test that the bottom is sound and the eggs won't fall out. Then they just lay
their eggs on the bare sticks or the rubble at the bottom of a tree hole.

A female Red-tailed Hawk built this nest one year and raised her family. The following spring, a female Great Horned Owl took over the empty nest.

Great Horned Owls accept many different kinds of nest sites. This female chose a hollow tree.

Though most owls choose high nest sites—in trees, on cliffs, or in buildings—two North American owls have the unusual habit of nesting on the ground. Short-eared Owls, which live in grassland habitat, just make a scrape on the ground within a concealing clump of vegetation. It's not clear whether the female lines this nest with grass or whether grass just gets mashed down by her nesting movements.

Snowy Owls, which breed in the treeless arctic tundra, also nest on the ground. An owl will choose its nest site with the defensive eye of a military strategist. Though the tundra landscape is generally flat, most Snowy Owl nests are on a slight rise—such as a hummock or boulder—that provides a good view of the surroundings. An elevated spot is also advantageous when the snow melts because low ground may flood. Snowy Owl nests also tend to be located with 100 yards of a body of water, where densely sprouting vegetation creates habitat for their rodent prey.

Burrowing Owls are unique among owls—and unusual among birds—for their habit of nesting underground. These little owls move into the abandoned burrows of ground squirrels, prairie dogs, and badgers.

Birds that build cup nests have to make a new nest each year. A pair of owls may use the same tree-hole or snag-top nest site year after year. On the other hand, the loosely constructed stick nests of raptors and crows aren't all that sturdy, so owls don't usually return to these sites for a second use.

Barn Owls, which mate for life, tend to have a very strong affinity for their nest site, even using it outside the breeding season. When one member of a

A red-phase Eastern Screech-Owl finds this wooden nest box to be a fine place to roost during the winter. Directions for building a nest box can be found in Chapter 7.

Barn Owl pair dies, the other takes a new mate and keeps the nest site. In this way, a nest site may be continuously occupied by Barn Owls for decades.

Laying and Incubating the Eggs

Most birds lay eggs that are oval, like the familiar chicken's egg. Owls, in contrast, tend to lay round eggs. And though bird eggs come in a rainbow of colors, all owls lay plain white eggs.

These two traits are related to the owl habit of nesting in enclosed spaces. Round

Left: *Tundra-dwelling Snowy Owls nest right on the ground. They are fiercely protective of their owlets.*

Below: *Burrowing Owls get their name from their habit of nesting underground. They don't usually do their own digging, however. They move into abandoned rodent burrows—or sometimes evict the owners.*

eggs pack closer together than oval eggs, so they fit better in a small enclosed space. Oval eggs have the advantage of rolling around less than round eggs, however, and Snowy Owls and Short-eared Owls, which nest on the ground, lay eggs that are more oval-shaped than those of most owls.

Owl eggs can be white because they're well hidden and well protected. White stands out in most natural environments—it contrasts with green and brown—so birds that have open, unprotected ground nests, such as killdeers and plovers, lay dun, speckled eggs that blend with the background. But inside a tree hole or woodpecker cavity, or high in a crow's nest, an owl's white eggs are well hidden from sharp-eyed predators. And if a raccoon or snake does try to steal eggs, owl parents, with their strong beaks and talons, are better equipped than the average songbird to drive the intruder away.

The female owl lays one egg every one to three days, until the clutch is complete. The number of eggs in an average clutch varies from species to species, but five eggs is typical. (More detailed information on typical clutch sizes is given in the species accounts in chapter 5.)

You might expect bigger owls to lay more eggs and smaller owls to lay fewer eggs, but this trend does not hold. Instead, some species, notably Barn Owls and Snowies, have large clutches in years when rodent populations are high and food is plentiful, but small clutches when rodent populations are low. It's a bit of a balancing act: the female uses a lot of energy laying each egg, and the male spends a lot of energy hunting for the family. It's only worth spending this energy on a large clutch if the chances are good that a lot of the chicks will survive.

Among the nine thousand or so known bird species around the world, in about 80 percent of all species, male and female parents share the job of incubating the eggs, sitting on them to keep them warm. With owls, however, the female usually does the job solo. Meanwhile, the male hunts for two and brings food home to her. It's not total confinement for the female; she does leave the nest each day for a few minutes to defecate, cough up a pellet, and stretch her wings.

The female starts to incubate right after the first egg is laid. The total amount of time she spends incubating is about four weeks, more or less. Some small owls have a shorter incubation period—just three weeks for Elf Owls—whereas the massive Great Horned Owl incubates for five weeks.

The owl habit of starting to incubate as soon as the first egg is laid is an uncommon strategy in the bird world. In most bird species, the female delays starting incubation until her clutch is complete—until all three or five or however many eggs are laid. It doesn't hurt the first-laid eggs to lie around unheated for a few days; meanwhile, delayed incubation ensures that all the chicks will hatch out at the same time. They'll all be the same size, and they'll all be ready to leave the nest together.

It's different with owls, which begin incubation right away. This is a particularly adaptive strategy for owls nesting early in spring in cold climates, where the first-laid eggs would freeze if the female waited before starting to incubate.

Because incubation starts with the first-laid egg, the eggs all hatch on different days. It can take as much as two weeks (or even longer, with a large clutch) from the time the first egg hatches to the last. This means that a nestful of owlets may include the owl equivalents of teenagers, preteens, toddlers, and infants.

Scientists think that these stair-step clutches may act as a kind of natural insurance policy. After all, the owl parents are engaged in a reproductive gamble. Their natural instinct is to try to raise as many young as they possibly can, but they can't predict from year to year whether they'll be able to find enough food to support a large clutch. With a stair-step clutch, in years when food is abundant, the parents will be able to feed even the last-hatched chicks. In lean years, the older, more robust chicks will grab most of the food, and the runts will starve. It may sound coldhearted to us, but it's not conscious or deliberate on the part of the owls—it's just nature's way of making sure that owl populations survive.

Raising Chicks

Once the eggs have hatched, the female may eat the eggshells and so recover the calcium they contain. Or the white eggshells may be carried off and dropped far from the nest so they don't attract the attention of predators.

The new-hatched chicks wear fluffy coats of white or gray down feathers. At first, they can't generate enough body heat to stay warm on their own. The female broods her owlets, keeping them warm by crouching over them. She makes a little tent, with the underside of her body for a roof and her drooped wings for the sides. The male continues to bring food to the mother and her young; she rarely leaves the nest, except to defecate.

When the little owls are bigger, better feathered, and able to generate their own body heat, the females of some species may leave the nest at times to help the males hunt for food. As the young owls get bigger, the two parents range farther and farther from the nest in search of prey.

It's typical among owls for the female to be significantly larger than the male. Some scientists think this size difference may be helpful to the pair when both are hunting for prey to feed their young. They can divide up the work, with the big female catching large prey and her mate catching smaller prey. This way, they're able to make the most of the resources in their territory.

Opposite page, top: *Most birds delay incubation until all the eggs are laid; this means that they all hatch at the same time. Owls, however, start incubating just as soon as the first egg is laid. This means the first egg may hatch a day or two before the next egg laid, and so on. The fuzzy coat of down is typical of newly hatched owlets.*

Opposite page, bottom: *A female Great Horned Owl feeds her chicks. The male brings home prey, which the female processes into bite-size bits for her youngsters.*

At first, young owls are too small to swallow a mouse or rat whole and headfirst. So the female prepares their meals, delicately tearing bits of meat with her beak. As the young owls grow, she gives them larger mouthfuls.

With as many as a dozen owls crammed into a small space, you might wonder about nest sanitation. Among Barn Owls, at least, when the owlets are very small, the female consumes their feces. In some species, the young owls instinctively void over the edge of the nest, helping to keep it clean for a while. But eventually the nest becomes a smelly mess.

Leaving the Nest

The time it takes for an owl to go from a hatchling to a fledgling—a young bird capable of flight—varies from about four weeks for the smallest species, such as Elf Owls and pygmy-owls, to nine or ten weeks for Great Horned Owls. Young owls have a lot to learn, though: how to hunt, how to stay safe. So even after they are big enough to leave the nest, they continue to hang around with their parents at the nest site for a while.

One unusual thing about owls is that in many species, the young leave the nest before they can actually fly. Tree-hole nesting owls usually do this. The

Notice the assortment of sizes in this brood of owlets. The largest owlet hatched from the first-laid egg; the smallest owlet hatched from the last-laid egg. In a good year, the parents will be able to feed the entire brood, but if prey are in short supply, the younger owlets will starve as the bigger, stronger owlets grab the food brought to the nest. This may seem cruel to us, but it's nature's way of ensuring that owls will raise as many offspring as conditions permit.

DOUBLE CLUTCHING

All animals naturally behave in ways that help them produce as many offspring as possible. Many common songbirds, including your familiar backyard visitors, such as bluebirds, cardinals, and sparrows, boost their reproductive output by raising not just one, but two or more clutches each year.

Owls, on the other hand, rarely double-clutch. The probable reason for this reproductive restraint is timing. Most owls take a fairly long time to raise a brood—longer than most songbirds. It takes a House Sparrow or Eastern Bluebird just about five weeks to go from new-laid egg to hatchling to free-flying fledgling. The same developmental steps take fifteen weeks—three times as long—for a Great Horned Owl. And then, even after the fledgling owl leaves the nest, it still hangs around with its parents for quite a while longer, often well into the fall, while the adult owls continue to feed and protect it. What all this means is that by the time young owls are capable of living independently, there isn't enough good weather left in which the parents could start raising a second owl family.

Barn Owls are the exception to the owl rule of one clutch per year. If their prey happen to be plentiful that year, Barn Owls may manage to nest twice, especially in areas with mild weather, such as California. Captive Barn Owls that don't have to work for their food have been known to manage as many as three clutches in a single year.

young birds get so big that they just don't fit in the hole anymore, so they clamber out onto some big branches in the nest tree and hang out there—sometimes for weeks—while their parents continue to feed them and their feathers continue to grow. Owls at this stage of development are referred to, appropriately, as branchers.

Branchers may fall from their perches to the ground, but they're not totally helpless. With effort, they may be able to scramble up the trunk, using their sharp talons and beak, until they reach a perch that is high enough to be safe from predators.

Once the young owls can fly—and catch food on their own—the parents start to force independence upon them. They ignore begging behavior and may even do a little aggressive chasing. Ultimately, the young owls wander off to find their own territories. This behavior is called dispersal. How far the young owls disperse varies from species to species, but a distance of 50 to 100 miles is pretty typical.

Life is hard for young owls. They have to leave their familiar home territory and find food in a new place, and they're not yet very skillful hunters. Some starve. Some are taken by predators. Some get shot by gun owners who don't know—or ignore the fact—that all owls are protected under the Migratory Bird Treaty Act. All too many die in collisions with cars or power lines. It's estimated that 50 to 70 percent of all owls die before they are a year old. Yet as long as populations are not gravely disturbed by human actions, enough owls survive to sustain the species.

5

Species Identification

This chapter includes an illustrated field guide to eighteen owl species that breed in North America. (A nineteenth species, the Whiskered Screech-Owl, is not pictured here because it's found mainly in Central America. In North America, its range extends into just a tiny corner of southeastern Arizona.)

Tips for Identifying Owls

Some species of birds are so distinctive that you can identify them at a glance. Male Northern Cardinals are bright red with crested heads; American Crows are big and black. Other birds are not so distinctive. About three dozen species of sparrows occur in North America, and most of them are small and brown—hard to tell apart without careful study.

As for owls, it's easy enough to tell that a bird is an owl by its overall shape and appearance: the upright posture, the large round head, the big eyes that face forward, and the formidable beak and talons. You can also tell an owl by its habits, as most live in forests, are active at night, and hoot or screech rather than sing.

But exactly what species of owl have you spotted? That question can pose some challenges. A number of owl species are similar in shape and color and can be tricky to tell apart. Still, if you approach owl identification in a systematic way, it's reasonably easy make an authoritative ID.

Voice

Most owls are active mainly at night, so chances are you'll hear an owl before you ever see it—if you see it at all. Luckily, each owl species has a unique and distinctive voice. This means you can identify owls by their calls alone.

In the Resources section, you'll find information about audio field guides: tapes, CDs, and websites that will help you learn to identify different owls by voice. One thing to remember when using audio guides is that although most owls have quite a repertoire of calls—to stay in touch with a mate, express alarm, frighten intruders, announce their arrival at the nest—most audio guides don't offer this entire repertoire. The typical audio guide only provides each species' primary call—the call most often made by a male owl, typically to defend his territory or attract a mate. So it is possible you'll hear sounds you can't identify with a guide. In that case, keep looking for the owl.

Size

If you can see an owl, its overall size is a useful clue to its identity. Is this owl large, medium-size, or small? Only three North American owl species are seriously big: the Great Horned Owl, Great Gray Owl, and Snowy Owl. All of these are about the size of a Red-Tailed Hawk (the big, bulky raptor often seen sitting in a tree by the highway).

Medium-size owls, such as the Barn Owl and Northern Hawk Owl, are about as big as a Cooper's Hawk or a crow. The smallest owls—the Elf Owl, pygmy-owls, and screech-owls—range from sparrow- to robin-size.

As you flip through the field guide included in this chapter, notice the owl size icons. You can use these icons to tell at a glance whether the owl being described is small, medium-size, or large.

Location

Another clue to an owl's identity is where you see it. Some owls have only a limited distribution. The Elf Owl, for example, is found only in the extreme southwestern United States and down to central Mexico. So if you see an owl that you think looks like an Elf Owl and you're in Michigan, it's almost certainly *not* an Elf Owl. Eastern and Western Screech-Owls look a lot alike, but each species is found almost exclusively on its own half of the continent. If you're owl-watching in Connecticut and you see a little gray owl, it's almost certainly an Eastern Screech-Owl, not a Western. (Apart from location, the best way to tell these two species apart is by their calls, rather than their appearance.)

Owls do wander, however—some more than others. Snowy Owls breed on the arctic tundra, but during winters when they can't find enough food because lemming populations are low, some Snowies will wander south and can wind up in such unexpected locations as Massachusetts and even Georgia. So yes, you could see an owl in a place where it wouldn't ordinarily be expected. Other species known for their winter wandering habits include Boreal Owls, Northern Saw-whet Owls, Northern Hawk Owls, and Great Gray Owls.

Field Marks

The late artist and naturalist Roger Tory Peterson produced the first pocket guide that systematically used field marks as aids to bird identification. Peterson's guide came out more than seventy years ago, and even though it was

during the Great Depression, when money was tight, the revolutionary little book sold out instantly.

Before Peterson, many so-called bird guides presented readers with long laundry lists of features to help you identify each species. The problem was, many of the features listed were visible only if you were holding the bird in your hand. Inspired by his bird-watching buddies, Peterson focused on traits that are easy to see at a distance, either with the naked eye or through binoculars—features such as stripes or bars on the wings, rings of color around the eyes, bars on the tail, and so on. A variety of field marks are useful for identifying owls.

Plumage color and pattern. Most owls are a mottled brown-gray overall. The Snowy Owl is an exception—it's white.

Check the color and pattern of the feathers. Start with the feathers on the back, chest, and breast. Do they appear to be marked with spots or lines? What color or colors are these marks? Are they white, black, or brown? If the marks look like lines rather than spots, are they streaks (vertical) or bars (horizontal)?

Sometimes careful observation of feather markings is all you need to make an ID. Spotted Owls and Barred Owls are about the same size, shape, and color, and they sometimes live in the same places—but Spotted Owls have spotted feathers, whereas Barred Owls have bars on the upper chest.

Also look at the bird's facial disk. Is it round or heart-shaped? Is it pale or dark? Is it bordered with a ring of contrasting color? Are there other distinctive marks on the face? A Barn Owl's white, heart-shaped face is unmistakable. The Great Gray Owl seems to wear a mustache.

Bars on the tail (or lack thereof) are another field mark that can be used to sort out certain species. Also check whether the crown of the head is streaked or spotted. And check the back of the neck, where Northern Pygmy Owls, Ferruginous Pygmy-Owls, and Northern Hawk Owls have white "eyespots."

Ear tufts. Some owls have prominent ear tufts; others have small ear tufts; and still others have none. So ear tufts can be another diagnostic field mark.

Consider Great Gray Owls and Great Horned Owls. They are about the same size and can sometimes be found in the same forests. But it's easy to tell them apart, because the Great Gray has a round head and is gray in color, whereas the Great Horned has prominent ear tufts and is more brown in color.

Just remember that owls that do have ear tufts sometimes hold these feathers down flat—when they are irritated, for example, or as they fly. So what looks like a round head may actually be tufted and just temporarily sleek.

Owls come in all sizes, from big as an eagle to small as a sparrow. To give you a sense of the size range, here's the largest owl in North America—the Great Gray Owl—sitting next to an Elf Owl, the smallest owl. (You'd never see these birds together in nature— the Great Gray lives in northern forests, while the Elf Owl prefers desert habitat.)

Eye color. Most North American owls have bright yellow eyes. A few species have dark (brown or black) eyes: the Barred Owl, Northern Spotted Owl, Barn Owl, and Flammulated Owl. So if you're close enough to get a good look, eye color can be a very handy clue to an owl's identity.

If you're in an eastern forest and you see a large owl with dark eyes, it's likely a Barred Owl, not a Great Horned Owl with its ear tufts laid flat, because Great Horned Owls have yellow eyes. If you're in a western forest and you're lucky enough to see a small owl with dark eyes, it's almost certainly a Flammulated Owl; Western Screech-Owls look similar but have yellow eyes.

Beak color. Owl beaks come in a variety of drab colors, from ivory to yellow to olive to black. Eastern and Western Screech-Owls look much alike, and there is an area in the middle of the United States where their ranges overlap. But Eastern Screech-Owls usually have pale bills, and Westerns usually have dark bills. So beak color may help you to distinguish between the two.

Color Phases

In Toronto, Canada, most of the eastern gray squirrels are actually black. In Florida, some Great Blue Herons are actually white. When a species exists in more than one pelt or plumage color, scientists call these different options color morphs or color phases.

If you see an owl that's familiar in shape but unusual in color, check the guide to see if the species occurs in more than one color phase. Several different owls exhibit color phases. Eastern Screech-Owls have both a gray and a red phase (really it's more of a cinnamon brown), as well as an intermediate mix of colors. Flammulated Owls also exist in red and gray phases. Most Western Screech-Owls are gray, but there's also a brown variant. Barn Owls have white and orange phases.

COOL COLORS

In northern areas, gray-phase Eastern Screech-Owls predominate; in southern areas, red-phase owls are more common. Why the difference between northern and southern populations? Scientists aren't sure, but one study showed that red-phase owls were more likely to die during sudden cold snaps. A follow-up lab study showed that in temperatures lower than 23 degrees F, red-phase owls had to burn more energy in order to keep themselves warm than gray owls did, suggesting that they were at a disadvantage in cold climates.

It's still not clear why gray-phase screech-owls are more energy-efficient and better at keeping warm than red-phase owls. One possibility is that gray feathers have, for some reason, more insulating power than red feathers. Another possibility is that feather color is genetically linked to some other trait that helps owls keep warm.

Male versus Female

How can you tell whether a bird is male or female? With many songbirds, you can tell a bird's gender by its plumage. Warblers are good examples: The male, at least in mating season, has far flashier plumage than the female—the better to attract her attention.

Among owls, males and females usually look much alike, at least as far as feather color and pattern goes. Owls that are active during the day, and so rely on vision as much as hearing, do show some differences in appearance. Snowy Owls live in the Arctic, where summer days last twenty-four hours; males are almost pure white, whereas females have dark markings. (Apparently the filmmakers who worked on the Harry Potter movies didn't know or didn't care about this tidbit of owl biology: Harry's owl, Hedwig, is supposed to be a female Snowy, but an all-white male owl was cast in the role.)

Although male and female owls of the same species generally look alike, one way they often differ is in their size. Female owls are usually larger *and* heavier than male owls. This kind of size difference is unusual among birds as a group. In 90 percent of all bird species, and in most mammals, males are larger than females. For females to be larger than males is quite common in the animal kingdom as a whole, however—among fish, frogs, turtles, snakes, and arthropods in particular.

Great Gray Owls, Snowy Owls, and Great Horned Owls are some of the species where the size difference between the sexes is so great that if you see an owl in the field, you may be able to guess whether it's male or female based on its size. In many other owls, though, the size difference is slight. You'd need to put the owl on a scale or measure it with calipers to tell if it is male or female.

Burrowing Owls are unique among North American owls: males of this species are actually larger than females.

Species Accounts

Each owl species in the field guide section of this book is identified by two names: a common name and a scientific name. Common names are the names that ordinary people use in everyday speech: Great Horned Owl or Burrowing Owl, for example. In the United States, these common names are written in English. In other countries, the common name is written in the national language.

Scientific names are the names scientists use. They may be Latin, Greek, or both, or based on Latin or Greek. The scientific name for the Great Horned Owl is *Bubo virginianus;* for the Burrowing Owl, *Athene cunicularia.* Carolus Linnaeus, a Swedish biologist, developed the scientific naming system in 1758. He chose Greek and Latin for scientific names because these were languages studied by most educated Europeans of the time.

Why did Linnaeus feel the world needed a scientific naming system? One reason is that scientific study transcends national borders. With a standardized system for naming living creatures, scientists who speak different languages can be sure they are talking about the same species.

Consider the Barn Owl: It's found on every continent except Antarctica, and in every nation, it has a different common name. To the French, it's *chouette effraie;* in the Carib language, it's *oeloekoeleja;* to the Dutch, it's *kerkuil;* in Russian, it's *sipukha;* in Japanese, it's *men-fukuroo.* Scientists in every nation, however, know this owl as *Tyto alba.*

Another reason scientific names are useful is that over time, some species accumulate more than one common name. Someone who knows the Arctic Saw-whet Owl might assume that Richardson's Owl is a different species. But actually, both are common names for *Aegolius funereus,* also known as the Boreal Owl.

Scientific names are always made up of two words. The first word in the name identifies the owl's genus; the second identifies the owl's species.

A species is the basic unit of biological classification. In general, a species is a group of organisms that all share a unique set of characteristics. They look alike, they sound alike, they act alike. Members of the same species mate with one another and produce fertile offspring.

A genus is a group of closely related species. For example, Barred Owls, Spotted Owls, and Great Gray Owls are all unique species, but all are members of the genus *Strix,* also known as the wood owls.

Each species in the field guide is accompanied by an icon to aid in field identification. The icons have the following meanings:

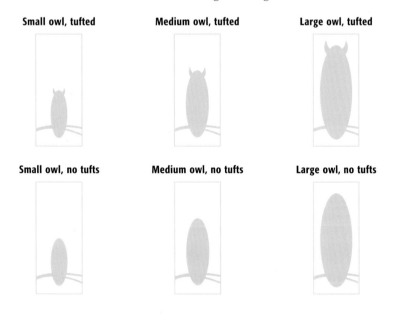

| Small owl, tufted | Medium owl, tufted | Large owl, tufted |

| Small owl, no tufts | Medium owl, no tufts | Large owl, no tufts |

The table below gives English-language names for some common owl genera (the plural of genus) and explains what traits the members of each genus share in common.

Genus	Commonly known as	Description
Tyto	Barn Owls	Heart-shaped facial disk
Otus	Flammulated Owls	Small owls; slender; small ear tufts; highly nocturnal
Megascops	Screech-owls	Small owls; have ear tufts; plumage looks like tree bark; do not actually screech
Bubo	Eagle owls and Snowy Owl	Large, powerful owls; most have prominent ear tufts
Surnia	Northern Hawk Owl	Falconlike; long tail; small facial disk
Glaucidium	Pygmy-Owls	Small owls; often day-active; prey mostly on insects
Micrathene	Elf Owl	The world's smallest owl
Athene	Burrowing Owl	Small owl; lacks ear tufts; long-legged
Strix	Wood owls	Big, round, obvious facial disks; lack ear tufts; live in forests
Asio	Eared owls	Hunt in open habitat; roost in groups
Aegolius	Forest owls	Small owls with big, rounded heads; lack ear tufts; typically live in large tracts of forest

Barn Owl *(Tyto alba)*
Barn Owl Family (Tytonidae)

About the name: The genus name, *Tyto,* is from the ancient Greek, meaning "night-owl." The species name, *alba,* is Latin for white and refers to the ghostly pale breast and belly. The common name, Barn Owl, comes from this species' habit of nesting in barns and other buildings.

Size: Medium. Worldwide, Barn Owls vary quite a bit in size and appearance; North American Barn Owls are the world's largest, however. Females range from 13^1/$_2$ to 15^1/$_2$ inches long; males are slightly smaller, at 12^1/$_2$ to 15 inches.

Distribution: This is one of the world's most widely distributed land birds. Barn Owls can be found on every continent except Antarctica, though not in very cold regions. They are found throughout the United States, except for the northernmost central states and northern New England.

Description: Barn Owls are easy to recognize. Most are white-phase birds and have pale feathers overall: white on the breast and belly and light gray-brown on the back. Orange-phase birds have tawny or buff-colored underparts. Either way, the back is marked with fine, dark lines and speckled with tiny, white spots. The dark eyes contrast with the pale, heart-shaped face. Other features to note are the lack of ear tufts and the unusually long legs. Females tend to be darker in color than males.

Look-alike species: This is only owl in North America with dark eyes in a pale, heart-shaped face. In flight over its grassland hunting grounds, a pale-colored Short-eared Owl might be mistaken for a Barn Owl—at least in the areas where both are found.

Habitat: Open woodlands and countryside. Small, old-fashioned farms provide perfect habitat—a mix of open fields where the owls can hunt, and hedgerows, woodlots, barns, and outbuildings where they can roost and nest.

Vocalizations: The Barn Owl doesn't hoot. Instead, it screeches—often while flying. The eerie quality of its voice has earned it nicknames like "devil's owl" and "ghost owl."

Feeding habits: These are night hunters. Voles and mice are typical prey, but Barn Owls also take small birds, insects, frogs, small lizards, baby rabbits, and rats. They often hunt on the wing by coursing, flying low and slow, back and forth, over open fields.

Distinctive behaviors: Instead of flying in a direct line, Barn Owls tend to swing from side to side. This species does not make regular migrations; however, in some years, large numbers of northern Barn Owls may move south for the winter, probably because prey is in short supply.

Nesting habits: In places where nest sites and prey are plentiful, Barn Owl pairs may nest close together. They often nest in barns, silos, church spires, attics, mine shafts—any place that is sheltered, quiet, and accessible. A good roof is a valuable resource in rainy climates, since a Barn Owl's feathers are not very waterproof. Before humans were around to provide buildings as nest sites, Barn Owls nested in tree holes. This species adjusts breeding efforts to local conditions, with females laying more eggs—or even raising a second clutch—in years when prey is abundant. A clutch is typically four to seven eggs but may be as large as fifteen. Sometimes a female starts laying her second clutch while owlets from the first clutch are still in the nest.

Flammulated Owl *(Otus flammeolus)*
Typical Owl Family (Strigidae)

About the name: In Greek mythology, Otus was one of Poseidon's sons. He was sentenced to spend eternity in Hades, chained to his brother, with a Screech-Owl perched on their chains. *Otos* is Greek for "ear," and the Greek naturalist Aristotle used the term *otus* to refer to any owl with ear tufts. The species name, *flammeolus,* is Latin for "flame-colored" and refers to the reddish streaks on this owl's shoulders and back.

Size: Small. In fact, this is the second-smallest owl in North America (the Elf Owl is the smallest). Flammulated Owls measure 6 to 6^1/$_2$ inches long, with a 14-inch wingspan (that's about one-quarter the size of Great Horned Owls, which see them as snack food). Male and female are the same size.

Distribution: Flammulated Owls are secretive in their habits and hard to spot, but they're widely distributed in the western mountains of North America, from southern British Columbia down to Mexico, in the Sierra Nevada and Cascade ranges and the Rocky Mountains. Migratory populations winter as far south as the highlands of Guatemala and El Salvador.

Description: This owl's dark eyes are a distinguishing trait; all other small North American owls have yellow eyes. Though all members of the genus *Otus* have ear tufts, a Flammulated Owl's tufts are small and hard to see in the field. Individuals that live in northern forests dominated by Douglas fir, which has gray bark, tend to have gray-brown plumage and no flame streaks; owls in southern forests, where Jeffrey pines have red bark, tend to have cinnamon-tinted plumage. Either way, subtle mottling of the feathers provides perfect camouflage against the bark. The breast and belly are lighter in color but have dark marks that look like pencil scribbles.

Look-alike species: The Western Screech-Owl has yellow eyes and more prominent ear tufts.

Habitat: Flammulated Owls like forests with big, old trees where woodpeckers have already been at work making nest holes. They also like an open understory, which makes it easy for them to capture flying insects on the wing.

Vocalizations: They may be small, but their deep voices make these owls sound big. A male defending a territory gives a distinctive call: a short, one- or two-note hoot that some naturalists translate as *poop* or *poip.*

Feeding habits: Active only at night, Flammulated Owls eat almost nothing but insects. They glean beetles, spiders, and moths from tree bark or pine needle clusters, or catch insects in flight.

Distinctive behaviors: This is one of just a few North American owls that migrate. Unfortunately, living in such remote areas, they are hard to study, so there's not much data on where different populations go in winter or what paths they take.

Nesting habits: The best nest site is a tree hole pecked out by a Pileated Woodpecker or Northern Flicker. The female usually lays just two or three eggs, which hatch in twenty-two to twenty-four days. The young fledge at twenty-two to twenty-five days old, but their parents continue to feed them for about five more weeks.

Western Screech-Owl *(Megascops kennicottii)*
Typical Owl Family (Strigidae)

About the name: The ancient Greeks had several words for "owl," but *scops* is the one they used most often. The species name, *kennicottii,* honors Maj. Robert Kennicott, a nineteenth-century naturalist who collected the first specimen of this little owl for science in the 1860s while accompanying a telegraph survey to "Russian America," today's Alaska.

Size: Small. Males are about 8 inches long, with a 21-inch wingspan. Females are slightly larger, about 9 inches long, with a 22-inch wingspan.

Distribution: These owls are found from southern coastal Alaska and coastal British Columbia south through the western United States to southern Baja California and the Mexican highlands.

Description: Most of the small owls in North America are round-headed, with no ear tufts, but the Western Screech-Owl has large ear tufts that are conspicuous when held erect. These owls come in two main color phases, gray and red (actually more of a dull cinnamon), as well as intermediate color phases. Red-phase birds live only in the humid Pacific Northwest. Whether red or gray, the mottled light-dark pattern of the feathers closely resembles vertical furrows in tree bark. The eyes are yellow, and the bill is black with a pale tip.

Look-alike species: Western Screech-Owls look much like their close cousins, Eastern Screech-Owls; indeed, taxonomists once considered the two a single species. The two overlap only in eastern Colorado and south Texas, so those are the only places where you'll have to work to tell them apart. The western species can be identified by its dark bill; eastern owls have yellowish or greenish bills. Or listen for the distinctive call (see Vocalizations below).

Habitat: One of the most common western owls, this species is found from Alaska to Mexico. Western Screech-Owls accept a range of habitats, but they favor open, deciduous woods at low elevations. You can also find them in parks and suburban backyards with suitable trees.

Vocalizations: Despite their name, these owls do not screech. The best-known vocalization is the male's territorial call: a quick series of short hoots that are spaced closer and closer together as the call continues. Think of how a bouncing Ping-Pong ball sounds—slow at first, then faster and faster.

Feeding habits: Active at night, Western Screech-Owls are classic sit-and-wait hunters that take many different kinds of prey. For populations in cold climates, the menu changes with the seasons; the owls take mostly insects in warm weather, mostly small mammals and birds in winter. Though they are small, they are fierce. When they have young to feed, they sometimes tackle prey much larger than themselves, such as young chickens, ducks, or grouse.

Distinctive behaviors: A perched Western Screech-Owl that feels threatened stretches tall and sits very still, perfectly imitating the stub of a broken branch. Maneuvering through the woods after prey, these owls fly like bats, darting and dodging to avoid colliding with trees.

Nesting habits: A pair may return year after year to the same nest site, typically a natural tree hole or woodpecker hole in a deciduous tree such as an oak or cottonwood. Owls in Arizona often nest in giant saguaro cacti. Western Screech-Owls also use nest boxes in suburban backyards. The female may lay two to seven eggs; a clutch of three or four is most typical. After an incubation period of twenty-six to thirty days, the young remain in the nest for another twenty-eight to thirty-five days.

Eastern Screech-Owl *(Megascops asio)*
Typical Owl Family (Strigidae)

About the name: In his *Dictionary of American Bird Names,* Earnest Choate says the name screech-owl is "rather a libel on this bird," because it actually gives a "liquid, wavering whistle" rather than a screech. Writing in the first century, the Roman natural historian Pliny the Elder used the word *asio* to mean "an owl with ear tufts."

Size: Small. Males average 8¹/₅ inches long, with a 21-inch wingspan. Females are slightly larger: 9¹/₅ inches long on average, with a 22-inch wingspan.

Distribution: These owls live in the United States east of the Rocky Mountains. Small populations extend north into southern Canada and south into Mexico.

Description: Eastern Screech-Owls come in three main color phases: gray, red, and brownish birds that are intermediate between red and gray. Gray-phase birds are most common in the North and in south Texas, whereas red-phase birds are most common elsewhere in the South. The eyes and bill are yellow. The ear tufts, conspicuous when erect, are sometimes held flat.

Look-alike species: The Western Screech-Owl looks quite similar but has a darker bill and somewhat shorter ear tufts. You can also tell Eastern and Western owls apart by their different-sounding calls.

Habitat: These owls live mostly at low elevations and occupy many kinds of habitats, including both disturbed and pristine forests, with both evergreen and deciduous trees, although they avoid dense forests where predators such as Great Horned Owls lurk. They are perfectly happy in suburban and even urban backyards as long as big trees provide nest cavities—or homeowners offer nest boxes.

Vocalizations: In the breeding season, males and females stay in touch with a muted, one-note trill. They use a distinctive descending trill or tremolo that sounds like a whinnying horse to defend the nest or territory.

Feeding habits: If the Great Horned Owl is the "flying tiger," this is the "flying bobcat." The Eastern Screech-Owl is fierce for its size and takes a wide variety of prey: small rodents, songbirds, reptiles, amphibians, insects, crayfish, earthworms, and more. Basically, if an animal is small enough for this owl to catch, it's fair game. These owls are most active just after dark. They are sit-and-wait hunters, but when they launch from a perch, they are often pursuing insects, which they catch on the wing with their beaks.

Distinctive behaviors: Eastern Screech-Owls are known to deposit live blind snakes in their nests. These very small snakes feed on fly larvae and other pests that thrive in a messy owl nest.

Nesting habits: Males really know how get a female's attention. First they bow, raising the wings while bobbing and swiveling the head. Then they do a full-body bob. They accentuate their message with a series of slow winks. The best nest site is a natural cavity in an oak, maple, or elm tree, but woodpecker holes are acceptable. The female may lay two to eight eggs; three or four is typical. Eastern Screech-Owls are unusual in that the male sometimes takes a turn sitting on the eggs, which hatch in about thirty days. The young fledge at about thirty days old.

Great Horned Owl *(Bubo virginianus)*
Typical Owl Family (Strigidae)

About the name: The genus name, *Bubo,* comes from the ancient Greek for "large owl." Europeans settlers first saw this bird in the Virginia colonies, so naturalists of the day assigned it the species name *virginianus.* The common name is obvious: this is a great big owl with ear tufts resembling horns.

Size: Large and heavy. A Great Horned Owl can be 18 to 25 inches long, with a 5-foot wingspan, and may weigh as much as 4 pounds. Great Gray Owls are considered the largest North American owls because they are somewhat taller than Great Horned Owls (27 to 28 inches long), but Great Grays are much slimmer, rarely weighing more than 3 pounds.

Distribution: The most widely distributed owl species in North America, Great Horned Owls are found throughout the United States, Canada, and Alaska, except for the extreme north, and throughout Central and South America, except for the Amazon basin and the Andes.

Description: Most Great Horned Owls have mottled brown-and-buff feathers. Birds in humid coastal regions tend to be darker; desert owls are more pale. The massive body, prominent ear tufts, and white bib under the chin are distinguishing traits. Sometimes called the "flying tiger" for its catlike face and ferocious habits.

Look-alike species: Long-eared Owls are similar in overall appearance, with brown plumage and prominent ear tufts, but they are significantly smaller. Great Gray Owls are similar in size but are gray in color and have no ear tufts.

Habitat: These owls live in a wide variety of habitats. All they need is a safe place to roost during the day, such as a stand of conifers; a nest site, typically a hawk's abandoned stick nest; and a place to hunt.

Vocalizations: The male's territorial call carries for miles. It's a series of about five or six hoots that are loud and low-pitched, with the last two notes drawn out and descending. It sounds as if the owl is saying, *"Who's a-wake? Me, tooo . . ."*

Feeding habits: Great Horned Owls take more than 250 different kinds of prey, small and large, including insects, bats, mice, muskrats, rabbits and hares, gulls, geese, and even skunks. (Luckily, these owls have a poor sense of smell.)

Distinctive behaviors: These owls mostly hunt from perches but will also pursue prey on foot or wade into shallow water after fish. They've even been seen hawking after large, flying water beetles. Though this species is not migratory, young birds living in northern forests may wander south in winters when snowshoe hare populations are low.

Nesting habits: A courting pair will sing duets, preen each other, and do a kind of bowing dance. The female usually lays two to four eggs, which hatch after twenty-six to thirty-five days. The young leave the nest at about six weeks of age—before they can fly—to climb around on branches near the nest tree. They have good flight skills by nine or ten weeks but still rely on their parents for food well into the fall.

Snowy Owl *(Bubo scandiacus)*
Typical Owl Family (Strigidae)

About the name: This species was formerly classified in the genus *Nyctea,* meaning "of the night," a poor name for an owl that hunts in the endless sunshine of arctic summers. The species name, *scandiacus,* is from the Latin for Scandinavia, where these owls are common. The common name describes either the snow white plumage or this species' tundra habitat.

Size: Large and heavy. Measuring 20 to 27 inches long, with a wingspan exceeding 5 feet, Snowy Owls can weigh as much as 4^1/$_4$ pounds—heavier than Great Horned Owls and Great Gray Owls. Females are slightly larger than males.

Distribution: Snowy Owls live on the fringe of arctic habitat known as tundra, which circles the top of the globe, from northern Canada and Alaska to Siberia, Scandinavia, and Iceland. In winters when prey is in short supply, many Snowy Owls wander south; in North America, they have shown up as far south as central California, southeastern Texas, and Georgia.

Description: Big and white, these owls are unmistakable. Males can be pure white; females and juveniles have some dark markings. The eyes are golden, and the small ear tufts are usually not visible. The black bill and the toes and talons are practically hidden under a layer of insulating feathers.

Look-alike species: None. Snowies are unique.

Habitat: Most owls are forest birds; Snowy Owls emphatically are not. They breed on the treeless and mostly flat tundra, where vegetation includes lichens, grasses, small flowering plants, and dwarf shrubs. Owls that wander south in winter often show up in open spaces that resemble tundra, such as airports.

Vocalizations: Many owls vocalize year-round, but Snowy Owls are silent most of the time. Males give their deep, booming territorial hoots only in breeding season. The low-pitched sounds travel well across open spaces.

Feeding habits: During the breeding season, Snowy Owls are specialists: They hunt lemmings and voles, and that's about it. In winter, they go after other—and sometimes larger—prey, including rats, rabbits and hares, grouse, and waterfowl.

Distinctive behaviors: Snowy Owls scan for prey while perched atop rocks or natural hummocks, the most elevated perch sites they can find on the tundra. Though they don't make conventional migrations, in years when lemmings are in short supply some subset of the population wanders south looking for food—more owls in years when owl populations are large. These Snowy Owl invasions generate excitement among bird-watchers in the lower forty-eight states.

Nesting habits: The male shows off for a female with an undulating display flight, sometimes while holding a lemming in his beak. He continues the display when he lands, turning his back to the female and spreading his massive wings wide. A female that's intrigued will approach and demand a bite. The nest site is usually located on a high mound; eggs are laid right on the ground. If lemmings aren't abundant, the female typically lays three to five eggs; when food is plentiful, she may lay up to fourteen. Both parents protect the owlets with a distraction display in which they appear be injured or by hissing and snapping furiously. Young birds leave the nest at about twenty-five days old but don't learn to fly until about forty-five days old. According to one estimate, it can take as many as fifteen hundred lemmings to feed a single Snowy Owl chick from hatching to independence.

Northern Hawk Owl *(Surnia ulula)*
Typical Owl Family (Strigidae)

About the name: Nomenclature expert Earnest Choate thinks the genus name, *Surnia,* may be an arbitrary word invented by a nineteenth-century French naturalist. The species name, *ulula,* is Latin for "screech owl." The hawklike appearance and behavior are the source of the common name hawk owl.

Size: Medium-size. About 14 inches long, with a wingspan of $2\frac{1}{2}$ to 3 feet, and weighing 10 to 12 ounces.

Distribution: These owls live in the boreal forest zone that circles the North Pole. In North America, this runs from Alaska east throughout Canada to Newfoundland, and includes northern Michigan and Minnesota; in Eurasia, it extends from Scandinavia to Siberia.

Description: With its slim body, pointed wings, and very long, tapered tail, this owl looks like a hawk—except for its large, distinctively owl-like head. Its plumage is mostly gray and white overall. The round head is speckled with white, the dark back and wings are spotted with white, and the pale belly is marked with narrow, dark or reddish bars. Also look for thick black stripes on either side of the pale face. The eyes are yellow.

Look-alike species: Flying through deep woods or across open country, this owl is sometimes mistaken for an immature Cooper's Hawk. When the owl is perched, the large head is a dead giveaway.

Habitat: Northern Hawk Owls breed in northern forests of fir, spruce, and tamarack, or in mixed deciduous-conifer forests. They often hunt over recently burned areas, where tree stumps make good perch sites and new vegetation attracts prey. Outside of the breeding season, they may disperse from forests to more open terrain, such as fragmented forests or farms with plenty of trees.

Vocalizations: The male's territorial call is a musical twittering that sounds like the species' name: *ululululu . . .*

Feeding habits: During long summer days, these owls hunt in broad daylight. In winter, when days are short, they may also hunt after dark. Besides hunting from a perch, they will quarter in search of prey, flying low over open ground, and they may hover like a harrier before dropping on prey. They also plunge like Great Gray Owls to catch rodents tunneling under snow. Northern Hawk Owls take mostly voles and young snowshoe hares during the summer breeding season; they add birds, including large species such as grouse and ptarmigan, to their diet in winter.

Distinctive behaviors: Because they live in remote areas, most Northern Hawk Owls aren't afraid of humans, so they may allow a close approach and seem quite tame. As with Snowy Owls and Boreal Owls, some members of the population wander south in winter, at roughly three- to five-year intervals, when rodent populations crash and food is in short supply.

Nesting habits: Northern Hawk Owls nest in holes pecked out by the larger woodpecker species, such as Pileated Woodpeckers, in the hollow tops of dead trees, in nest boxes, and (rarely) in abandoned hawk nests. A male will sit near a nest site he's discovered and give his "advertising" call to let prospective mates know they should check it out. The female lays three to nine eggs; seven is typical. Incubation lasts twenty-five to thirty days. In the short northern summers, the owlets grow rapidly. They leave the nest when they are three weeks old, though their parents help them for another two months or so.

Northern Pygmy-Owl *(Glaucidium gnoma)*
Typical Owl Family (Strigidae)

About the name: The genus name, *glaucidium,* is the diminutive of a Greek word that means both "glaring" and "owl." The species name is from the Greek *gnome,* meaning "intelligence," a nod to Athena, the goddess of wisdom, who was often depicted with an owl. Northern refers to its distribution, and pygmy to its small size.

Size: Small. About 6 to 7 inches long, with a 15-inch wingspan. Females are larger than males.

Distribution: This is a bird of western mountain forests. Its range extends south from southern Alaska along the major mountain ranges in two long fingers. One reaches down the West Coast to California and Central America; the other extends southeast to Colorado.

Description: A small, plump, round-headed owl with a long, narrow tail. The plumage is gray, gray-brown, or cinnamon-tinted overall, with tiny white spots on the head, shoulders, and wings, and dark, vertical streaks on the white breast. On the nape of the neck are two oval-shaped black spots, edged with white, which look like eyes on the back of the head. The actual eyes are yellow, topped with white eyebrows, and the bill is pale yellow.

Look-alike species: The Ferruginous Pygmy-Owl is similar in appearance, except that its head is streaked, not spotted, but the two species live in different places. Their ranges overlap only in a small part of southern Arizona, and there the Northern Pygmy-Owl lives at higher elevations. You can also tell the two apart by their vocalizations.

Habitat: Northern Pygmy-Owls can be found in a variety of mountain forests, usually near meadows or other open areas.

Vocalizations: The male advertises his territory with a monotonous *toot* or *toot-toot* repeated over and over.

Feeding habits: Versatile predators, these little owls take mostly small prey—small mammals, insects, and songbirds—but they also manage large targets, including quail twice their size. They hunt at dusk and dawn, occasionally by day, rarely at night, although this pattern can vary with elevation and location. In winter, they pile up sizable prey caches.

Distinctive behaviors: This species relies more on sight than sound to locate prey. Whereas most owls fly silently, the Northern Pygmy-Owl can be noisy in flight. Because forest hawks will attack it, this owl is adept at hiding in plain sight by sitting motionless. Most owls cast pellets after every meal; Northern Pygmy-Owls cough up very small pellets and only occasionally, because they're dainty eaters that usually pick meat off the bone instead of swallowing prey whole.

Nesting habits: Northern Pygmy-Owls have been known to share nest trees (though not the nest holes) with Northern Saw-whet Owls or Pileated Woodpeckers. The female lays two to seven eggs, typically three. Not much is known about this owl's nesting habits, but some observers think the female delays incubation until all the eggs are laid so that they hatch all at once.

Ferruginous Pygmy-Owl *(Glaucidium brasilianum)*
Typical Owl Family (Strigidae)

About the name: Brazil is one of the areas where you will find this species, hence the species name *brasilianum.* Ferruginous means "rusty-colored;" it's from the Latin word *ferrum,* meaning iron, which rusts.

Size: Small. About 6 to 7 inches long, with a 15-inch wingspan. Females are slightly larger than males.

Distribution: This is a southern species. In the United States, small populations are found in southern Arizona and Texas. Ferruginous Pygmy-Owls can be found south through Mexico and Central America to north and central South America, except for the Andes.

Description: This little owl is reddish brown or brown overall. Identifying features include a white breast marked with heavy brown vertical streaks; faint white streaks on the top of the round head, which has no ear tufts; and a long, dark tail marked with light brown to orange bars. Like the closely related Northern Pygmy-Owl, this species has black eyespots on the nape of its neck; its real eyes are yellow, with white feathers above that look like scowling eyebrows.

Look-alike species: The Northern Pygmy-Owl, which also occurs in southern Arizona, is similar but has white bars on its tail (rather than brown or orange bars) and has spots, not streaks, on its head. The Elf Owl, which also occurs in Texas, is a little smaller and more gray in color, with a shorter tail. It also lacks the black eyespots and hunts only at night

Habitat: This species lives at lower elevations and in drier habitats than the Northern Pygmy-Owl. In Arizona, which is the only place both kinds of pygmy-owls occur, you're most likely to see Ferruginous Pygmy-Owls around saguaro cactus or the mesquite thickets that sprout on riverbanks.

Vocalizations: The male's advertising call sounds like the Northern Pygmy-Owl's *toot-toot,* but speeded up. If the female is around, she may reply with a chittering call.

Feeding habits: Hunting by day and night, this species, like other small owls, takes mostly insects, including grasshoppers, crickets, and caterpillars. It also catches birds, small mammals, little lizards and frogs, and will even tackle prey larger than itself, including rats, quail, and (rarely) domestic chickens.

Distinctive behaviors: This owl is most active at dawn and dusk. It likes to find a perch near a thicket and make sallies out to grab insects.

Nesting habits: Like many small owls, Ferruginous Pygmy-Owls most often nest in woodpecker holes, either in trees or—most picturesquely—in saguaro cactus. They also nest in natural tree cavities, forks of trees, tops of stumps, or holes in sandbanks or termite mounds, and they will accept nest boxes. The female lays two to five eggs (typically three) and incubates them for twenty-one to twenty-three days. The young fledge at twenty-six to twenty-eight days old, but the parents help them out for another three weeks.

Elf Owl *(Micrathene whitneyi)*
Typical Owl Family (Strigidae)

About the name: The genus name, *Micrathene,* combines the prefix *micra,* meaning "small," with Athena, the Greek goddess of wisdom, to whom owls were sacred. The species name honors geologist and explorer Josiah D. Whitney, who in the 1860s helped map the new state of California (the state's Mount Whitney was also named for him). The common name refers to this owl's diminutive size.

Size: This is the world's smallest owl, no more than 6 inches long and weighing 1 1/2 ounces tops. It can fit easily in the palm of your hand. Females are a little larger than males.

Distribution: The southwestern border of the United States is the northern edge of this owl's range. It can (just barely) be found in Southern California, southern Arizona, and the southwest edge of Texas. From there, its range extends south into Mexico.

Description: Elf Owls are brown-gray overall, with white dots on the forehead and wings. The tail is very short, with pale horizontal stripes. Other field marks include a round head with no ear tufts, white belly, cinnamon-tinted face, and white collar on the nape. White eyebrow feathers arch over yellow eyes.

Look-alike species: Where their ranges overlap, you might confuse the Elf Owl with the Northern or the Ferruginous Pygmy-Owl, but the pygmy-owls are bit larger, have longer tails, and are active by day, rather than at night

Habitat: Elf Owls can be found in deserts with saguaro cactus, thornbushes, or mesquite, and also in forests along ravines, canyons, and mountain slopes. They seem to be adapting to urban areas.

Vocalizations: These owls don't really hoot. The male's advertising call is a high-pitched *yip-yip-yip-yip-yip,* like a little dog yelping. When the moon is bright, he may go on all night.

Feeding habits: Night hunters, Elf Owls have small, weak feet. They catch crickets, beetles, moths, scorpions, spiders, and centipedes, and often hawk out from a perch to nab prey on the wing. About the size of bats, they have a similar darting flight and will come to campfires or floodlights to catch the insects swarming around the light.

Distinctive behaviors: Elf Owls process their prey carefully, stripping inedible wings from moths and pulling stingers from scorpions. Northernmost populations migrate south for the winter, but little is know about the timing or path of these movements.

Nesting habits: Other owls use nest holes pecked out by large woodpeckers such as Pileated Woodpeckers or Northern Flickers. These petite owls use the smaller holes drilled by acorn and ladder-backed woodpeckers. Elf Owls favor holes in saguaro cactus, perhaps because the thorns repel predators. When the male finds a good hole, he goes inside and calls loudly. Then, when an intrigued female approaches, he flies out with a flourish, still calling. The female lays one to five eggs, typically three. She incubates them for about twenty-one to twenty-four days; the young fledge at twenty-eight to thirty-three days old.

Burrowing Owl *(Athene cunicularia)*
Typical Owl Family (Strigidae)

About the name: Here's another owl named for Athena, the goddess of wisdom. The species name, *cunicularia,* comes from the Latin word for "rabbit" and means "one who burrows," but though these owls do nest in burrows, they don't usually do their own digging.

Size: Small (but larger than a pygmy-owl or Elf Owl): about 8^1/$_2$ to 11 inches long, with a 20- to 24-inch wingspan, and weighing 6 to 7^1/$_2$ ounces.

Distribution: This species is found in the grassland regions of western North America and south through Central America to the grassland regions of South America. Small populations of a Burrowing Owl subspecies occur in Florida and some Caribbean islands.

Description: The very long legs are distinctive. This owl's plumage is brown overall, with white spots on the back and dark marks on a white breast. The round head lacks ear tufts, and the eyes are yellow with white eyebrow markings. Burrowing Owls are unusual among owls in that males are as big as or bigger than females.

Look-alike species: The Burrowing Owl's behavior and habitat are so distinctive that you're not likely to confuse it with any other species. If you see a little owl standing on a fence post on the open prairie in broad daylight, it's probably a Burrowing Owl.

Habitat: Flat, open grassland, as well as deserts and farm fields—but only if burrowing mammals live there too. These owls nest almost exclusively in underground burrows dug by prairie dogs, gophers, ground squirrels, foxes, and badgers.

Vocalizations: The male's territorial defense call is a double hoot with a lilting, wide-open-spaces quality, a bit like a Killdeer's cry. Frightened chicks make a sound like a rattlesnake, which may discourage would-be predators from investigating burrows.

Feeding habits: These owls will hunt by day if that's what it takes keep their young fed. In winter, they hunker in burrows by day and hunt at night. They are versatile hunters and will run down grasshoppers, snatch dragonflies on the wing, or hover and then stoop on small mammals. Beetles are the most common insect prey.

Distinctive behaviors: Some people call them "howdy owls" for the way they bob their heads; they're actually trying to get a better look at prey, not nod hello. The male stands guard on an elevated perch—usually a fence post or mound of earth—near the nest site. He also maintains satellite burrows near the nest, where he sleeps. Most Burrowing Owls are year-round residents, but northernmost populations are migratory.

Nesting habits: These owls sometimes move into abandoned burrows, but they will also evict prairie dogs to claim a nest site. Though most owls are solitary nesters, Burrowing Owls often nest close together. Perhaps there's safety in numbers, or perhaps they simply have to nest wherever burrows are available. Also, though most owls do little or no work to spruce up the nest, Burrowing Owls will scratch out dirt to enlarge the burrow and line the entrance with cattle dung, feathers, or dog droppings (see page 34). The female may lay one to twelve eggs; six or seven is typical. She sits on them for about thirty days, while the male stands guard when he's not off hunting. The young leave the nest at about seven weeks of age.

Spotted Owl *(Strix occidentalis)*
Typical Owl Family (Strigidae)

About the name: The genus name, *Strix,* come from the Greek *strizo,* meaning "to screech," although taxonomically this species is not a screech-owl. *Occidentalis* is Latin for "western"; this owl lives exclusively in western North America, whereas its close relatives the Barred Owl and Great Gray Owl are more widely distributed.

Size: Medium-size. Females average 19 inches long, with a 43-inch wingspan, and top out at 1³/₄ pounds. Males are just a little smaller.

Distribution: There are three subspecies of Spotted Owls. Northern Spotted Owls range from British Columbia south along the coastal mountain ranges to central California. Mexican Spotted Owls occur from southern Utah and Colorado south through Arizona, New Mexico, and northwest Texas. The California Spotted Owl lives on the western slopes of the Sierra Nevada.

Description: Stocky and chestnut brown overall, Spotted Owls get their name from the bold, irregular white spots scattered over their feathers. This is one of just a few owls in North America that have brown, not yellow, eyes. The buff-brown facial disk, ringed with dark brown, is another distinctive feature. The female has a darker head than the male. There are no ear tufts.

Look-alike species: Barred Owls are very similar to Spotted Owls in size and body shape, but instead of spots, they have bars on the breast and streaks on the belly.

Habitat: Old-growth forests, where trees are more than two hundred years old, typically on mountainsides and in humid coastal zones. Old-growth forests are dense and shady, advantageous because this owl has very thick plumage and can overheat in summer. The big, old trees can accommodate big nest holes, and the relatively open understory makes hunting easier.

Vocalizations: Males and females defend their territories or keep in touch with a series of four to five mellow, widely spaced hoots that sound like *"Whooo are you? . . . you-all?"* An alarm call sounds like a dog barking.

Feeding habits: Night hunters, Spotted Owls are also classic sit-and-wait predators. In northern areas, they take mostly flying squirrels; in southern areas, mostly wood rats. In both places, they also take rabbits, birds, and some reptiles and invertebrates.

Distinctive behaviors: Spotted Owls enjoy drinking from and bathing in forest streams. They don't migrate in the conventional sense, but birds in the Sierra Nevada move downslope in winter.

Nesting habits: These owls often nest in abandoned Northern Goshawk nests. Thick clumps of mistletoe also make good nest sites; tree holes and cliffside caves are other alternatives. A pair may return to the same site year after year. The female lays two to four eggs, typically two, and incubates them for twenty-eight to thirty-two days. At five weeks old, the young clamber from the nest onto nearby tree branches. They start to fly about a week later—sooner than most branchers. It's another three to four weeks before they can hunt for themselves.

Barred Owl *(Strix varia)*
Typical Owl Family (Strigidae)

About the name: The species name, *varia,* is Latin for "variegated," which itself means "having streaks, marks, and patches of various colors." That's a perfect description of this owl's markings. Barred refers to the dark horizontal bars on the upper breast.

Size: Variable; individuals can be medium-size to large. Barred Owls range from about 16 to 25 inches long, with a wingspan of 38 to 50 inches, and can weigh 1 to 2 pounds. Females are about 10 percent longer than males.

Distribution: Barred Owls are common throughout the eastern half of North America, from Florida up to southern Canada. From there, their range extends westward to Washington State and then south to northern California. A subspecies lives in central Mexico.

Description: Like its close relative the Spotted Owl, this is a round-headed, stocky brown owl with brown eyes. The pale facial disk is marked with four or five concentric rings of darker feathers. The dark horizontal bars on the throat and upper breast contrast with dark vertical streaks on the belly.

Look-alike species: Barred Owls do resemble Spotted Owls (and the two sometimes interbreed, producing "Sparred" Owls), but except for the Pacific Northwest, the two species aren't found in the same places.

Habitat: Barred Owls nest in a variety of habitats, from expansive tracts of large mature trees to narrow wooded corridors along riverbanks. They often claim territories near open areas where the hunting is good, especially swamps, wetlands, and lakes.

Vocalizations: Males and females keep in touch with a distinctive nine-note call that sounds like *"Who cooks for you, who cooks for you-all?"*

Feeding habits: Night hunters, Barred Owls sometimes start prowling before sunset if the day is dark or their chicks are very hungry. They hunt from perches and take mostly small rodents, including voles, shrews, and deer mice, along with squirrels, young rabbits, and other small mammals. Barred Owls sometimes hover when searching for prey but don't hunt on the wing; they take small songbirds after the birds have settled on nighttime roosts.

Distinctive behaviors: These owls stick to their home territories. They don't migrate, and they only rarely wander south in winter looking for food, as some northern owls do. Their versatility as hunters ensures a steady food supply year-round. A pair will use the same nest site year after year.

Nesting habits: Large owls need large tree holes as nest sites. That's why Barred Owls are found in forests with big, old trees, or even small forest patches with just one big tree. An abandoned hawk, crow, or squirrel nest also makes an acceptable nest site, though Barred Owls in tree holes raise more young than owls in stick nests. The female lays two to four eggs, typically two, and incubates them for twenty-eight to thirty-three days. The young leave the nest at four to five weeks old to clamber around the nest tree; they master flying a week or two later. The parents look out for them for another four months—the longest known period of parental care of any owl.

Great Gray Owl *(Strix nebulosa)*
Typical Owl Family (Strigidae)

About the name: The species name, *nebulosa,* is Latin for "clouded," describing feathers the color of a storm cloud and also the blurry-edged, indistinct spots. Great refers to its large size.

Size: Large. The Great Gray is the largest—or at least the tallest—owl in North America, 28 inches on average for females, 27 inches for males, with a wingspan of more than 5 feet. Great Grays tend to be lighter in weight than the other large owls (Great Horned and Snowy), but a female in February, bulking up for the breeding season, can weigh more than 3 pounds.

Distribution: These are northern owls with a circumpolar distribution. In North America, they're found from Alaska across Canada, and also south to the northern Rocky Mountains and northern Minnesota, Wisconsin, and Michigan. They also inhabit the northern latitudes of Europe and Asia.

Description: Dark gray overall, with light gray and white markings. The head is unusually large in proportion to the body, and the yellow eyes are comparatively small. The round head has no ear tufts. The very large, pale facial disk is marked with six or more concentric dark semicircles. White feathers between the eyes take the shape of two back-to-back Cs. The yellow bill stands out against a patch of black feathers that looks like a little goatee.

Look-alike species: The Great Horned Owl, which is similar in size and lives in some of the same places (and sometimes preys on Great Grays), is browner in color and has big, obvious ear tufts.

Habitat: Great Gray Owls live in boreal and montane forests—that is, northern evergreen forests of spruce and fir. To find a Great Gray Owl territory, look for an expanse of mature forest next to an open meadow.

Vocalizations: The male's territorial call is a slow series of soft, low-pitched hoots.

Feeding habits: This species hunts at all hours but especially at dawn and dusk. Though big enough to take large prey, such as snowshoe hares or Spruce Grouse, the Great Gray specializes in taking small rodents, mostly voles. In winter, when voles and mice are hidden in tunnels beneath the snow, Great Grays can locate them by sound alone and plunge through the snow to make a capture.

Distinctive behaviors: Flying looks like an effort for Great Gray Owls, which flap like giant moths. In winters when food is scarce, or when a very hard snow crust makes it impossible to plunge after voles in their tunnels, some owls move far south of their usual range. Extra long, fluffy feathers help Great Grays keep warm in winter, but in summer they risk overheating, so they pick the shadiest roost spots.

Nesting habits: After some mutual preening and courtship feeding, the male calls to invite the female to check out a nest site; she sits there and scrapes her feet, as if trying it out. The female lays two to five eggs, typically three, which she incubates for twenty-eight to twenty-nine days. The young leave the nest at three to four weeks old. After another four weeks of scrambling around in the nest tree, they are ready to fly. The parents help them out for several more months. In the breeding season, Great Gray Owls do not defend a hunting territory around their nest sites, the way some owls do. For this reason, Great Grays sometimes nest very close together, particularly when prey are abundant. This concentration of nests may be why Great Gray parents sometimes feed chicks that are not their own.

Long-eared Owl *(Asio otus)*
Typical Owl Family (Strigidae)

About the name: This owl's tall ear tufts are so conspicuous that taxonomists paid homage to them twice when bestowing a scientific name: *Asio* is the Latin word used by Pliny to mean "an owl with ear tufts," and *otus* is a Greek word meaning the same. It's called long-eared for the same reason.

Size: Medium-size. Females are about 14¹/₂ inches long on average, with a 39-inch wingspan. Males are about 13¹/₂ inches long, with a 38-inch wingspan.

Distribution: Long-eared Owls are widely distributed across the United States, except in Florida and along the Gulf coast; they also breed across southern Canada. Their distribution extends to similar latitudes in Europe and Asia. There are isolated populations in North Africa and the Canary Islands.

Description: This slim owl has brown and buff plumage mottled with black and gray. Three distinctive traits are the tall ear tufts, the orange-brown facial disk, and the white chin patch. The eyes are golden yellow. Females tend to be darker than males.

Look-alike species: Great Horned Owls resemble Long-eared Owls in overall shape and color, but are twice as big. A Long-ear in flight, when the ear tufts are not so visible, might be confused with the closely related Short-eared Owl, but Long-eared Owls are darker.

Habitat: Long-eared Owls usually choose dense woods for roosting and nesting, but they need open spaces nearby where they can hunt—ideally, open space studded with perch trees. Farmland with hedgerows, golf courses, cemeteries, and open land along rivers make good hunting grounds.

Vocalizations: The male's courtship call is series of low-pitched hoots, with fairly long pauses between hoots. The alarm call may sound like a barking dog or shrieking cat.

Feeding habits: Long-ears hunt mostly at night, though owls at high latitudes sometimes hunt during the long summer days to feed their hungry broods. They often hunt on the wing, flying low, just a few feet above the ground, looking down, the better to listen for scurrying deer mice or voles. Once an owl is locked onto a target, it stalls in midair, then drops feetfirst to make the grab.

Distinctive behaviors: When startled, Long-eared Owls adopt a tall concealment pose that makes them look almost impossibly slim. They don't snow-plunge like other northern owls, so populations in northern areas often migrate south in winter to reach areas where snow is not so thick and food is more accessible. Long-eared Owls have the unusual habit of roosting communally in winter, with groups of seven to fifty owls sharing a tree. Some individuals may return to the same winter roost year after year.

Nesting habits: The male does a courtship display flight that involves noisy wing clapping. Abandoned stick nests, well hidden by dense foliage, are preferred for nesting. The female may lay two to ten eggs, typically four to five. She incubates them for twenty-five to thirty days. The young owls climb out on branches around the nest tree about three weeks after hatching and start flying two weeks later.

Short-eared Owl *(Asio flammeus)*
Typical Owl Family (Strigidae)

About the name: The species name, *flammeus,* means flame-colored. The common name comes from the fact that its ear tufts are far smaller than those of the closely related Long-eared Owl.

Size: Medium-size, typically 13 to 17 inches long, with a 41- to 42-inch wingspan. Females are just slightly larger than males.

Distribution: In North America, Short-eared Owls winter in snow-free areas throughout the continent; they breed throughout Alaska, Canada, and the northern half of the continental United States. They are also found throughout South America (except for the Amazon basin), Europe, and Asia.

Description: These owls are a tawny buff-brown overall, with dark vertical streaks on the breast and belly. In flight, "wrist marks" on the undersides of the wings are conspicuous; they are black, bordered with pale feathers. The small ear tufts are not usually erect. Yellow eyes are ringed with dark feathers, as if the owl is wearing smudgy eyeliner. Females tend to be darker in color than males, and more streaky.

Look-alike species: The closely related Long-eared Owl is very similar in size and shape, but darker in color overall, with those big, conspicuous ear tufts.

Habitat: Whereas Long-eared Owls nest and roost in trees, Short-ears nest on the ground and usually roost there, too, taking to trees only when the ground is snow covered. So you tend to find Short-ears in open country: marshes, grasslands, prairie, farm fields, and tundra.

Vocalizations: This owl doesn't call much—but then, it's active by day in open habitat, where prospective mates can use visual as well as audible signals. The male's territorial advertisement call is a long series of *hoos,* which some people say sounds like an old steam engine. This call is often given as part of a flight display.

Feeding habits: Short-eared Owls hunt both by day and at night. Like Long-ears, they mostly hunt on the wing, flying low to the ground. If the hunter detects prey concealed in shrubbery or dense grass, it often hovers, facing into the wind, before making its move. Meadow voles are the preferred prey, but these owls also take other small mammals, such as deer mice, shrews, and ground squirrels, along with grassland songbirds. Short-ears in coastal areas often take shorebirds.

Distinctive behaviors: The mottled feathers make good camouflage, but if a Short-ear has been detected, it may play dead rather than flee. When perched, Short-ears hunch forward in a hawklike posture. Their mothlike, fluttering flight is also distinctive. At night, in summer, they roost on the ground, though Short-ears in desert areas may roost in rodent burrows. In winter, they roost in trees but—unusual among owls—roost communally, in groups of up to two hundred birds. They will also gang up to harass large birds such as eagles, hawks, turkey vultures, and herons. Birds in the northern part of the range migrate south to snow-free areas in winter.

Nesting habits: Of all the owls, this species has one of the most elaborate courtship rituals. It starts with the male's flight display, in which he pumps his wings to rise high in the sky, hovers, then swoops down and up, often while clapping his wings below his body and sometimes singing. To conclude the display, he raises his wings high and drops rapidly to earth. Short-eared Owls nest right on the ground, unusual for owls. The female scrapes a bare spot under a tuft of grass and lays one to fourteen (typically five to seven) eggs, which she incubates for twenty-four to twenty-nine days; the male sometimes helps out with nest-sitting. The young leave the nest as early as twelve days of age, though they can't fly till they are four weeks old. Groups of Short-eared Owls sometimes share good habitat by nesting close together.

Boreal Owl *(Aegolius funereus)*
Typical Owl Family (Strigidae)

About the name: *Aegolius* is yet another Greek word meaning "a kind of owl." The species name, *funereus,* may have been assigned with the idea that the call sounds like a funeral bell. Boreas was the Greek god of the north wind, and this owl lives in boreal (far northern) forests.

Size: Small. About 8 to 12 inches long, and weighing about 3 to 7 ounces.

Distribution: Boreal Owls live in boreal forests. In North America, they're mostly found in southern Alaska and across Canada, with some populations extending south along the spine of the Rocky Mountains. This species also occurs in the boreal forests of Europe and Asia, where it is known as Tengmalm's Owl.

Description: This round-headed owl has a dark brown back spotted with white, neat rows of white spots on its wings, more white spots on its dark forehead, and a white breast streaked with chocolate brown. The gray-white facial disk has a black border. The eyes are yellow, and the bill is pale.

Look-alike species: The closely related Saw-whet Owl is similar in appearance but is smaller, has white streaks (not spots) on its forehead, has a dark (not pale) bill, and is a lighter reddish brown in color.

Habitat: In the boreal forests where you'll find this owl, the dominant trees are spruce, aspen, poplar, birch tamarack, and fir. The species favors mature forests with a closed canopy that keeps out the sun, so the snow in winter doesn't develop an icy crust but stays soft. Because they are small, Boreal Owls can't punch through ice to get at rodents beneath the snow the way the more powerful Great Gray Owl can.

Vocalizations: The male's territorial call is given in a monotone. It's a short series of quick little hoots that run together, almost like a trill. He calls, waits a few seconds, then repeats, over and over. Each Boreal Owl has its own distinctive voice.

Feeding habits: These owls are active mostly at night. A Boreal Owl on the hunt will take up its position on a low branch, then sit quietly while moving its head slowly from side to side. It is scanning the ground, not with its eyes, but with its ears, listening for rodent footsteps in the undergrowth. Voles are the most common prey, but Boreal Owls also take lemmings, shrews, and other small forest rodents, plus the occasional small bird, frog, or beetle.

Distinctive behaviors: This owl's dense feathers are so warm that it's at risk for overheating in the summer. That's another reason Boreal Owls seek out the deepest, darkest spots in the forest, so that they can roost in cool shade. Like Great Gray Owls, Northern Hawk Owls, and Snowy Owls, Boreal Owls are known for their irregular winter wanderings into the lower forty-eight states. Birds that make the trek south are hungry, and many starve to death along the way.

Nesting habits: Woodpecker holes are the preferred nest sites, but biologists have discovered that they can attract these owls to convenient study sites by putting out nest boxes. Once a male owl finds a good nest site, he stocks it with prey, then hops onto a nearby perch to call loudly, inviting females to come and check out his offering. The size of the clutch can range from one to ten eggs (four to six is typical); the female will lay more eggs if prey is plentiful, and in very good years, an enterprising male may support two females. The eggs hatch after twenty-eight to twenty-nine days. The young leave the nest at thirty to thirty-two days old, though their parents continue to feed them for another month or so.

Northern Saw-whet Owl *(Aegolius acadicus)*
Typical Owl Family (Strigidae)

About the name: The eighteenth-century German naturalist Johann Gmelin dubbed this owl *acadicus* because the specimen he examined had been collected in the colony of Acadia, today's Nova Scotia. Some say the name saw-whet was bestowed because, to the ears of colonial settlers, this owl's alarm call sounded like a handsaw being sharpened on a whetstone.

Size: Small. Indeed, this is the smallest owl in the eastern United States, about 6$\frac{1}{2}$ to 8$\frac{1}{2}$ inches long, with an 18- to 22-inch wingspan, and weighing about 2$\frac{1}{2}$ to 4 ounces. Females are a little bigger than males.

Distribution: This owl is found only in North America, from coastal Alaska and the southern half of Canada through the United States to the central mountains of Mexico. A migratory species, the Northern Saw-whet Owl occupies the southern limits of its range only in winter, not in the breeding season.

Description: This owl's round head looks almost too big for such a small body. The legs are short, and the wings are long and rounded. Saw-whets are reddish brown overall, the feathers spotted with white on the back and streaked with white on the breast. The pale facial disk is edged with brown and white streaks that radiate outward like a sunburst, and the dark forehead is streaked with white. The bill is dark, and the eyes are yellow.

Look-alike species: The Northern Saw-whet's close cousin, the Boreal Owl, is a little larger and darker in color, has a spotted (not streaked) forehead, and a pale (not dark) bill.

Habitat: These owls inhabit both deciduous and coniferous forests where the understory includes plenty of tangles, shrubs, and thickets. They tend to pick nest sites in swampy areas.

Vocalizations: The male's courtship call is a monotone beeping that sounds like a mail truck's backup signal. Outside of the spring breeding season, Northern Saw-whets are mostly silent.

Feeding habits: These are classic sit-and-wait predators. They hunt mostly at dusk and dawn from low perches. Like Boreal Owls, they have sharp hearing and often hunt by sound alone. They catch mostly deer mice but will also take shrews, voles, and other small mammals, as well as small songbirds, frogs, and insects. Northern Saw-whet Owls often cache prey to eat later.

Distinctive behaviors: When perched, Saw-Whets tend to shuffle their feet. They're also very tame; if you see one, you can get quite close. Perhaps this is why people used to believe that owls were blind by day. This is one of the few owl species that makes regular migrations between northern breeding grounds and southern wintering grounds.

Nesting habits: Many owl species use the same nest sites and have the same mates year after year, but saw-whets do not; migration is full of dangers, and many owls do not survive the trip. Like most small owls, they nest mostly in woodpecker holes or natural tree cavities and will accept a nest box. If prey is abundant, a Northern Saw-whet male may be able to support a second female. A typical clutch has five to six eggs, which hatch after twenty-one to twenty-eight days. The young fledge at four to five weeks of age, but the parents help feed them for a few weeks more.

6

Watching Owls

Bird-watching is one of America's fastest-growing hobbies. According to the U.S. Fish and Wildlife Service, more than fifty million Americans call themselves bird-watchers. Experienced bird-watchers will tell you that owl-watching is a distinct—and particularly enjoyable—form of the sport. A nighttime trip in search of owls even has a special name: It's called an owl prowl.

Many local bird clubs, museums, and nature centers offer owl prowls. Usually these are midwinter walks, led by an expert owl-watcher. A typical owl prowl starts at sunset and lasts for an hour or two. Signing up for a guided prowl is a great way to get started watching owls. Check the yellow pages for a nearby nature center or science museum, or visit the birding websites listed in the Resources section of this book to find a local bird club. This chapter will help you go prowling for owls on your own.

When to Go

Most organized owl prowls happen from late fall to early spring—the breeding season, when owls are noisiest and therefore easiest to find. Males are calling more at this time, to defend territories and attract mates. Also, deciduous trees are leafless in winter, making owls easier to spot.

Summer can also be a productive time to look for owls. After young owls leave the nest, they often hang around in their parent's territory for weeks to months, enjoying continued protection and free meals while refining their hunting skills. When there's a bunch of noisy owls all hanging around in one place, they're pretty easy to find.

Whatever time of year you're searching for owls, you will rely on your ears as well as your eyes. Plan your prowl for a clear, moonlit night when the wind is still; a breeze makes it hard for you to hear owls, and it also prevents owls from hearing their prey, so they'll be less active. Some species are also sensitive to atmospheric pressure and won't call if the barometer is falling.

An owl prowl doesn't mean you have to stay up past midnight. Many nocturnal owls are most active right at dusk. They have just woken up from their long day's nap and are beginning to search for prey and mates.

If you don't like the thought of roaming the forest at night, several owl species are active in the daytime. Short-eared Owls usually hunt in late afternoon, and during the summer breeding season, they are widely distributed throughout North America. They're also easy to see, because Short-eared Owls hunt in the open, over fields, meadows, and wetlands. There's no guarantee that a meadow that hosts owls one year will be a home for owls the next year, however, as this species tends to wander.

The Burrowing Owl is another species that hunts by day (as well as night) in open habitat. You'll find it in the grasslands of Florida, the Great Plains, and the West. Look for the long-legged adults standing guard by day on elevated perches near their nesting burrow entrances.

During irruptions, the northern owls that wander south in winter when food is in short supply can be easy to find. When Snowy Owls, Great Gray Owls, Northern Hawk Owls, and Boreal Owls are wintering in unfamiliar territory, they tend to choose daytime roosts that are right out in the open, where they often attract crowds of excited bird-watchers. Many bird organizations have hotlines and listservs that will tell you where to find these wandering owls.

Where to Go

Wherever you live, it's likely that at least a few owl species live near you. Great Horned Owls can make a home almost anywhere, and screech-owls often adapt to suburban settings.

Before you head out on a nighttime owl prowl, it's a good idea to do some advance scouting by day. If you'll be following a trail, notice how it is marked and any landmarks. If you know the lay of the land, you're less like to trip over obstacles or get lost in the dark.

A good place to start your owl prowl is in edge habitat, where a forest bumps up against open space. Many owls roost by day in deep forest but move to more open areas to hunt at dusk.

In the woods, look for likely roost sites, such as a little island of pines in a forest of oak. Scan tree trunks for whitewash, a layer of accumulated owl excrement. Some species of owls tend to return to the same perch each day to roost, and when it's time to take off again, they defecate right before liftoff, lightening the load—and leaving their calling cards. Forest-dwelling hawks, such as Cooper's Hawks, also leave whitewash marks under their roosts, but hawk whitewash tends to look rather splattered, whereas owl whitewash seems more solid, less liquid, and may pile up on the ground in little heaps.

As you walk in the woods, keep an eye out for whitewash (owl droppings). It's a telltale sign that an owl spent the day roosting on a branch above.

While looking for whitewash, also scan the bases of trees for owl leftovers: feathers or bits of fur torn from a carcass, or little piles of owl pellets. If the pellets are fading gray and crumbly, they're old, but if they look moist and compact, they are probably recent. Look up and scan the biggest horizontal branches above the pellet pile carefully—perhaps you'll spot the pellet maker. Also look for tree holes where an owl might roost.

You may be able to locate owl sites just by asking around. Barn Owls often roost in barns and abandoned buildings. If you see a property that looks as though it might provide an owl roost site, ask the owner whether owls have been seen or heard in the area.

When prowling for owls, always respect No Trespassing signs.

Locating Owls

Once you've scouted a patch of likely owl habitat and you're out on a prowl, what do you do? Listen carefully. During breeding season, the male may move from perch to perch, pausing to call from each one. Or he may call to the female, inviting her to inspect a nest site. During the day, you might hear the sounds of a mob—a gang of smaller birds attacking an owl (see chapter 3).

Each owl species has a distinctive territorial call, which means you can identify an owl just by the sound of its voice. Just as you'd study a phrasebook before traveling abroad, study owl sounds before you go out on your prowl. An audio field guide—a CD or cassette tape with recorded owl sounds—is a useful tool for learning the different owl calls. You can also listen to owl sounds at certain websites. A list of audio guides and websites is provided in the Resources section.

Bird-watchers sometimes use a technique called playback to get birds to sing and reveal their location, or to entice birds out of hiding and within viewing range. This involves broadcasting recorded bird sounds in the field, using a portable tape player or CD player.

Playback works very well when owl-watching. Play the call of the species likely to be in the area, then turn off the recorder and listen for a few minutes. (Some owl-watchers don't bother with technology; they are skillful at imitating owl sounds on their own.) If an owl is in earshot, it will usually respond as soon as it hears the "intruder," and it may fly in and perch nearby. But sometimes you have to play a call repeatedly to get results.

If an owl responds but the sound is faraway and faint, try cupping your hands behind your ears or shifting your position to figure out what direction the call is coming from. Then work your way toward the sound, alternating between playback and listening.

While you are broadcasting, stay alert. Keep your eyes moving, scanning for motion; owls can fly silently, so you may not hear one land nearby. If you do see movement, you can use a flashlight to get a better look—but don't harass the owl by leaving it in the spotlight for too long. (In some states, it is illegal to spotlight wild animals, so check first with a conservation officer.) If no owl comes to your call, continue on your route and try again farther down the trail.

Owl-Watching Gear

Dress warmly in winter. Wear gloves and a hat, but not a furry hat that resembles owl prey, or you could be the target of a surprise attack. Wear sturdy, waterproof boots regardless of the season; forest trails can be muddy even after a spate of dry weather, and long grass gets wet with dew at night.

At night, carry a flashlight with fresh batteries. If you'll be bushwacking, also take along a map and compass or GPS, and make sure you know how to use these tools. It's a good idea to pack an emergency kit with water, high-energy snacks (you burn calories quickly in cold weather), waterproof matches, and a lightweight tarp. Carry your wallet with ID, in case the police stop to ask why you are parked in a lonely area or wandering down a forest road at night.

Binoculars can be useful even at night. To find binoculars that will work well in dim light, check the pair of numbers associated with each model, something like 7×35, 7×50, or 8×42. The first number in the pair refers to the

RARE BIRD ALERTS

Many bird clubs provide rare bird alerts. You can call a telephone hotline or check a website to find detailed information on where other people have seen rare or interesting birds.

If money is no object, you might want to consider a specialized service offered by the Houston Audubon Society: the North American Rare Bird Alert (NARBA). For a fee, you can arrange to have a NARBA volunteer call you personally whenever a species you particularly want to see (a wandering Great Gray? a Snowy?) is reported in your area. This service includes detailed directions on how to find the bird. See the Resources section at the back of this book for more information.

PROWLING TIPS

- *Be quiet.* Owls have sharp hearing and will avoid anything that sounds dangerous. Don't slam the car door as you get out. Keep your conversations to a whisper. Watch where you step so you don't snap branches or twigs or crunch dry leaves.

- *Move slowly.* Owls have sharp night vision and will avoid anything that looks dangerous. Slow movement makes you less conspicuous.

- *Use playback wisely.* Don't broadcast sounds more than a few times in one area. You could frighten an owl away from its territory if you sound like a competitor that won't give up. An owl that feels threatened also might attack you—and those talons can really do some damage.

- *Don't harass nesting owls.* If you find owls that are on a nest, take a quick look, then take off. Resist the temptation to check on the nest every few days. Nesting owls that are approached repeatedly may abandon their nests. Another risk is that predators may follow your scent trail and raid the nest.

magnifying power of the binoculars—how much bigger they make things look. The second number is more important for owl-watching: It refers to the diameter (in millimeters) of the objective lenses, the big lenses at the far end of the binoculars, away from your eyes. Larger objective lenses let in more light, which means the binoculars will work better in dim conditions. Binoculars with larger lens sizes such as 7×35 or 8×42 work okay in dim conditions; 8×26 compact binoculars do not.

Another factor to consider is the size of the exit pupil. Point the binoculars at a bright light, hold them at arm's length, and look through them. The circle of light you see in the eyepiece is the exit pupil. Because your own pupils dilate in dim light, you'll want a large exit pupil for night viewing. Check the specs on the binoculars: 7×35 binoculars have an exit pupil of 5 millimeters; 7×50 bins have an exit pupil of 7 millimeters and work very well in low-light conditions.

Owl-watchers who enjoy technology and have cash to spare may want to try military style night-vision binoculars, available from vendors who market to hunters.

If you plan to try playback to attract owls, also take along a portable tape player or CD player with fresh batteries, as well as a tape or CD of owl sounds.

Finally, if you are interested in collecting owl pellets to dissect, carry a plastic bag.

Dissecting Owl Pellets

You can discover what an owl has eaten by dissecting an owl pellet. Pellets contain the indigestible parts of an owl's prey: bones, fur, feathers, beetle wings and mandibles, and so on. Different species of small rodents have distinctively shaped teeth, skulls, and jawbones. So it's possible to tell what an owl ate by taking apart a pellet and examining these remains. It's interesting to do a comparative study with pellets from different species.

Owl pellets are not smelly or disgusting. You can either use pellets that you have found in the woods or order them from a biological supply house (see the Resources section). Purchased pellets usually have been sterilized. If you use pellets that you found yourself, it's a good idea to sterilize them first by one of two methods: Wrap the pellets in foil, place on an old cookie sheet, and bake in a 300-degree oven for an hour, then let cool; or soak them in a 10 percent bleach solution for a few hours. Soaking also will loosen the bones from the matted covering.

Here's what you'll need:

- owl pellet
- tweezers
- a couple of toothpicks or straightened-out paper clips to use as probes
- a surface to work on: a white paper plate, styrofoam meat tray, or other disposable, flat container
- 8× or 10× magnifying glass
- diagrams of rodent skeletons (see the Resources section)
- safety glasses
- dust mask
- latex gloves

Dissection is simple. Wearing safety glasses, dust mask, and latex gloves, use the tweezers and probes to gently tease apart the pellet. As you find small bones, set them carefully to one side. An empty egg carton makes a handy sorting tray. Depending on what kind of owl produced the pellet, you may find mostly bones and fur, feathers, or insect remains such as beetle wing cases, legs, and jaws. You may be able to identify the kinds of rodents by comparing any bones you've found to those on the diagrams of rodent skeletons.

When you are done with your dissection, be sure to disinfect your work surface, discard your gloves (don't reuse them), and wash your hands well.

Projects for Owl-Watching Volunteers

The field of ornithology has a long track record as a scientific discipline where amateurs make important contributions to research and discovery, working side by side with the experts. In keeping with that tradition, many owl research projects depend on the contributions of volunteers—members of the general public who are interested in owls and help out with fieldwork and data collection. The Resources section lists several owl projects that would love to have your help.

7

Nest Boxes for Backyard Owls

It's fun to go out on an owl prowl. But wouldn't it be great if you could watch owls from the comfort of your home?

One way you can do this is with technology. A number of websites have owlcams, videocameras that feed images from inside an actual owl nest. These webcams let you see the most intimate details of owl family life. The images may be updated on a regular basis or downloaded as videofiles.

But what if you want to see real live owls, up close and personal? You can't attract owls to your backyard the same way you attract songbirds, by putting out a bird feeder, but you can encourage owls to make a home in your backyard by putting up a nest box.

Many owls prefer to lay their eggs in dark, enclosed spaces: a tree hole, woodpecker hole, cave, or abandoned building. Nest boxes are just another kind of dark, enclosed space, and many species of owls will use them.

Owl nest boxes come in a variety of shapes, sizes, and materials. Most often, a nest box is just a plain wooden box, square or rectangular, with a round or square entrance hole. You can put an owl nest box on a tree, under the eaves of a building, or on a freestanding pole, depending on the preference of the species you are trying to attract.

Partly through research and partly through trial and error, scientists and owl enthusiasts have been investigating what kinds of nest boxes are most attractive to owls. Dimensions and instructions for building a Barn Owl or screech-owl nest box are given later in this chapter. For information on prefab, mail-order owl boxes, see the Resources section.

Owls scout around for nest sites before they mate. For the best chance of attracting an owl, hang your box out at least one month before breeding activity starts. Most owls start looking for nest sites and mates in midwinter to early spring, so autumn is a good time to put up a box.

Even with the nicest nest box, you won't attract an owl species that doesn't live in your area. Don't expect backyard Barn Owls if you live in North Dakota or Wyoming, or Northern Saw-whet Owls in Florida. Don't expect Eastern Screech-Owls in California, or Western Screech-Owls in New England. Check the species accounts in chapter 5 or the range maps in a bird field guide to find out what owl species live in your area.

To attract owls to your backyard, your yard must contain or butt up against owl habitat. And you must position the box in a way that meets the species' nesting requirements. Here are some details for attracting the kinds of owls most likely to use a backyard next box.

Species That Use Nest Boxes

Owls that are known to use nest boxes include the Barn Owl, Barred Owl, Boreal Owl, Burrowing Owl, Great Horned Owl, Great Gray Owl, Eastern and Western Screech-Owls, and Northern Saw-whet Owl. Of these, the two

NEST BOXES MAKE A DIFFERENCE

Besides being fun and interesting, nest boxes can be helpful to owls. In some cases, the size of an owl population is limited by a lack of nest sites. A forest that is comparatively young (because it was logged recently or is former farmland that has reverted to forest) doesn't have very many big, old trees—and usually it's the big, old, rotten trees that develop tree holes sizable enough for the big owls to nest in.

In suburban areas, homeowners religiously cut down dead or dying trees, before woodpeckers or natural decay can create the holes that owls need. So by providing nest sites for owls, you may help owl populations sustain themselves or even increase.

Nest boxes of a sort also have been deployed in an effort to help populations of Burrowing Owls. Researchers developed a kind of substitute burrow—a subterranean nest box—that these owls will accept. In some places where Burrowing Owl populations have been wiped out, these nest boxes have been installed in an attempt to encourage owls to move back in.

If you put up a backyard nest box, you can help owls in yet another way by collecting information on your tenants and submitting your data to the Cornell Lab of Ornithology in Ithaca, New York. This world-famous bird research center recruits citizen-scientists to help conduct many different projects. One is The Birdhouse Network (birds.cornell.edu/birdhouse/). To participate, you simply collect information on your nesting owls—how many eggs are laid and when, how many hatched, and so on—and send the data via the Internet to Cornell scientists. The data submitted is helping these scientists learn more about bird behavior and population trends. But please note: owls are very protective of their eggs and young. They won't hesitate to attack if they feel you are too close, and they'll aim for your face and eyes. So if there's nesting activity in your backyard box, give owls their space. Use binoculars to watch the action.

screech-owls and the Barn Owl are the most likely to use a backyard nest box. These owls seem comfortable nesting near buildings occupied by humans.

Boreal Owls will accept boxes that are placed in their habitat, but they are not exactly a backyard species, unless your yard adjoins a northern wilderness. Barred Owls will use boxes but prefer deep-woods habitat and sometimes abandon their nesting attempts if there's too much human activity nearby.

Nest boxes for Burrowing Owls are the most complicated to construct. They are installed underground, beneath a mound of dirt. Making homes for Burrowing Owls is a job usually tackled by state or federal wildlife biologists rather than individual homeowners.

Great Horned Owls will use a large or open-topped box, but they are less in need of a helping hand from humans. They often use platform nests, such as abandoned crow or hawk nests, so they have more nest site choices in nature.

Barn Owls

You may be able to attract Barn Owls if you live in an area with a mix of forest and open spaces. Your property should be away from heavily traveled roads and no more than half a mile from good owl hunting grounds, such as a pasture, hay field, marsh, golf course, or similar open area.

Barn Owls like nest sites that are fairly high up. Many sources recommend mounting a Barn Owl nest box 12 to 50 feet high. (That's quite a contrast to the typical bluebird box, which is usually mounted about 6 feet high.)

You can mount the box in a tree; under a gable on your house, barn, or garage; or on a tall post. Position the box so that the entrance hole faces out toward the hunting grounds (if you're not sure where the nearest open field is, face the entrance hole to the southeast). It also should face away from the prevailing wind and get some shade, not be in full sun all day. If you mount the box on a post or building rather than a tree, it should be within 100 yards of a large tree, as the young owls will need a place to branch when they first leave the nest. Barn Owls tolerate the routine noise and activity around a farm or home, but it's still best to place the box away from sidewalks and doors where there's a lot of foot traffic.

Don't put a Barn Owl box anywhere near where you park your car; owls defecate as they leave their nests to hunt, and their feces will corrode metal. And don't put the box near your bedroom window—Barn Owl chicks are very noisy at night when their parents deliver food.

Screech-Owls

If you live in a neighborhood where the real estate listings boast of "mature plantings," it's likely you can attract a screech-owl to your backyard nest box. In the wild, screech-owls prefer forest or woodlands that are close to a stream or swamp and have a subcanopy layer of shrubs below the tree canopy. They often choose nest sites in trees that are near the edge of a forest, close to an open area. An established suburban neighborhood, with its large shade trees, banks of shrubbery, and expanses of grassy lawn, is enough like this kind of natural habitat that screech-owls feel right at home.

In the wild, screech-owls nest in abandoned woodpecker holes. In addition to preferring nest sites that are next to a field or other open space, they look for nest holes that are in deep shade. The male stands guard outside the nest hole while the female incubates the eggs, and dense foliage helps him avoid the prying eyes of predators.

In light of these preferences, your best bet is to mount a screech-owl box below a good-size limb on a tree that is growing near an open area. Position the box 10 to 30 feet up the trunk and in the shade, with the entrance facing north. Choose a tree with a trunk wider than the box, and put an inch or so of dried leaves or wood shavings in the bottom of the box, to mimic the detritus in a woodpecker hole. Because owls won't bring nest materials to the box, some kind of substrate is needed to keep the eggs from rolling around. Screech-owls are so tolerant of human activity that some owl landlords have had success with boxes that are only 10 to 15 feet from the house.

Barred Owls

Not really a backyard species, Barred Owls might be attracted to a backyard box if you have a large property that includes deep woods (preferably a mature hardwood forest) and is near water. Barred Owls tend to choose a nest site within 200 feet of a river or lake.

Place the box in the woods, not on the edge of a clearing, at least 150 feet away from your house. The owls may abandon their young if they are bothered by human visitors more than a couple times per week. Mount the box on a large tree, at least 12 inches in diameter, near some sizable horizontal branches so the young owls will have a place to hang out after they leave the nest. Position the box so a passing owl can see the entrance hole—it shouldn't be obscured by branches or leaves. Put a layer of wood chips in the bottom.

Great Horned Owls

Like screech-owls, Great Horned Owls live in many kinds of habitat and can be found in suburban areas with mature trees. They sometimes nest in tree holes, but they're more likely to use a platform-type nest such as an old crow's nest. Thus if you really want to attract a Great Horned Owl, your best bet is to create a nesting platform, either by wedging an old tire in the fork of a tree or by building 2-by-2-foot flat wooden platform atop a pole at least 14 feet tall. Station the platform in an open area, but close to the edge of a woodlot.

Northern Saw-whet Owl

During the breeding season, these little owls can be found in bogs or swamps with stands of evergreen trees such as hemlock, spruce, or tamarack. If that describes your backyard, you're in luck. Saw-whet Owls ordinarily nest in tree cavities excavated by Pileated Woodpeckers or Northern Flickers. They prefer nest sites that are fairly high, usually more than 14 feet off the ground.

PUTTING UP A LARGE NEST BOX

Wooden nest boxes intended for the larger owls, such as Barn Owls and Barred Owls, as well as nest platforms for Great Horned Owls, are large, unwieldy, and very heavy. Mounting these structures on a tree or pole can be dangerous. You need a long ladder, and the heavy box must be supported in position while you bolt it to the upright support. If the box falls during this mounting procedure, it might injure people on the ground below. If you fall from such a height, you could be severely injured or even killed. Also, the platform or box needs to be securely mounted so that it won't get blown down in a storm, possibly injuring passersby or owls nesting inside the box.

So play it safe: call in a certified arborist or other professional who has the equipment needed to safely install your box or platform at the recommended height.

Nest Box Construction

There are nearly as many nest box designs as there are people who build them, and passionate arguments have been known to arise regarding the merits of one model over another. While this book can't hope to do justice to the wide variety of designs for each owl species, all nest boxes do have some basic features in common.

The instructions that follow are based on plans for a screech-owl nest box from the Minnesota Department of Natural Resources, but they can be modified for a number of species. Use the following table to adjust the dimensions of the box as necessary:

Species	Box floor (inches)	Box height (inches)	Entrance height (inches)	Entrance diameter (inches)	Placement height (feet)
Barn Owl	10×18	15–18	4	6	12–18
Barred Owl	14×14	12–23	8–12	7	15–20
Northern Saw-whet Owl and screech-owls	8×8	12–16	10–12	3	10–30
Great Horned Owl	24×24 platform or old tire				15–20

Begin by sawing your lumber as shown to create the pieces that will make up the box. In addition to the entrance hole on the front, predrill 1/4-inch holes in the bottom (for drainage), back (for easier mounting), and sides (for ventilation).

The bottom, top, back, and sides should be fastened securely together with nails or screws. The front piece, however, needs to pivot to allow for mounting and cleaning. To achieve this, drill a hole in the top front corner of each

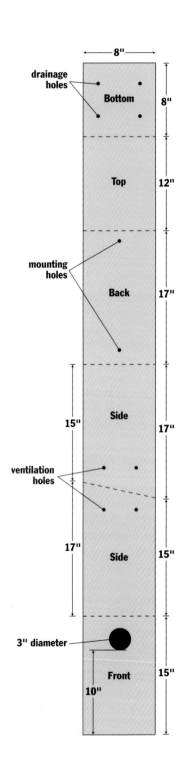

8"

drainage holes

Bottom   8"

Top   12"

mounting holes

Back   17"

Side   17"

15"

ventilation holes

17"

Side   15"

3" diameter

Front   15"

10"

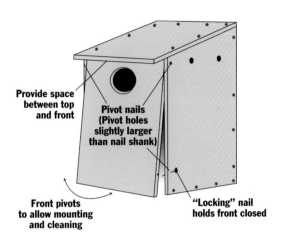

Provide space between top and front

Pivot nails (Pivot holes slightly larger than nail shank)

Front pivots to allow mounting and cleaning

"Locking" nail holds front closed

10'

Screech-owl nest box design courtesy of
Minnesota Department of Natural Resources

side—the point where the side will attach to the front—that is slighter larger than the nail (or screw) shank. This will allow the nail, and therefore the front, to swing freely. Be sure to leave a little space between the front and the top, or the front will be immobilized.

You'll need a third nail to make sure the front stays closed when you're not cleaning. Drill a hole near the bottom front corner of the side, through to the front piece, again slightly larger than the nail shank. You should then be able to insert and remove the nail with minimal difficulty.

Nest Box Maintenance

Ornithologists are still debating the merits of cleaning out nest boxes after the young birds fledge. Intuitively, it seems as though cleaning out the detritus after the nesting season would get rid of pests and parasites. Yet in controlled experiments, chicks raised in boxes where the old nests were left in place were no more pest-infested than chicks raised in cleaned-out boxes.

One argument against cleaning out nest boxes is the risk of contact with deer mice. In many western states, some deer mice are infected with hantavirus. This virus is present in mouse droppings and urine, and it can be deadly if inhaled. Many owls eat deer mice, which means that mouse parts may be strewn about the box. Also, live deer mice often move into nest boxes after the birds move out.

If you choose to clean out your nest box and you live in an area where hantavirus is present (check the CDC website, www.cdc.gov), wear rubber gloves

ABANDONED BABY OWLS

You find a young owl on the ground, calling loudly. What to do? If the owlet seems healthy and isn't obviously injured, its parents are probably nearby and taking care of it by bringing food and protecting it from predators. Even though it goes against your instincts, you must back off and leave the owlet alone so its parents can do their job.

If the young owl is clearly injured and needs medical care, don't try to administer first aid yourself. It's not just that owls are tricky to care for, or that their sharp beaks and talons could hurt you—it's also against the law. Under the provisions of the Migratory Bird Treaty Act, only licensed professionals may possess or handle a wild bird. You need to call a wildlife rehabilitator for help.

It's also important to realize that you won't be doing the owl any favors by trying to care for it. Owls raised by people become imprinted on them and cannot be returned to the wild.

To locate a wildlife rehabilitator, check the yellow pages under "wildlife," call your local animal shelter or nature center, or contact your state department of fish and game, wildlife, or natural resources.

and a dust mask. Wait until you are sure the last owlet has fledged. Disinfect the box interior by spraying with a 10 percent bleach solution, one part bleach to nine parts water. Let the solution soak in for twenty minutes before you try to remove the debris inside.

Whether or not you clean the nest box, it's a good idea to take a peek inside the box in the fall, before adult owls start looking for nest sites, to make sure the box hasn't been taken over by paper wasps or bees. Check on a cold day, when insects won't be active. If you find an insect nest, you can use a putty knife to scrape it out. Or you can use pyrethrin, a natural insecticide made from flower petals, to kill the bees or wasps. If wasps are a recurrent problem, try coating the inside ceiling of the box with soap; it will discourage wasps from starting a nest.

RESOURCES

Books about Owls

North America

North American Owls: Journey through a Shadowed World, by Jim Burns. Minocqua, WI: Willow Creek Press, 2004.

The author traveled all around North America in order to observe all nineteen North American owl species. Each chapter is a thoughtful essay on a species. A CD showcasing the owls' voices is part of the package.

North American Owls: Biology and Natural History, by Paul A. Johnsgard. Washington, DC: Smithsonian Institution Press, 2002.

This is *the* authoritative scholarly monograph on North American owls. It's rather readable for a work intended for scientists. And it is just one of many fascinating books about birds by distinguished ornithologist and author Paul Johnsgard, a professor emeritus of the University of Nebraska.

Owls: The Silent Flyers, by R. D. Lawrence. Buffalo, NY: Firefly Books, 2001.

Written for bird enthusiasts rather than for scientists, this book includes species accounts and color photographs for all nineteen species of North American owls.

Owls, by Floyd Scholz and Tad Merrick. Mechanicsburg, PA: Stackpole Books, 2001.

Lavishly illustrated with color photographs and line drawings, this book by renowned woodcarver Floyd Scholz presents sixteen North American owls, focusing on anatomy and behavior. There's also a how-to section on carving and painting.

The Birds of North America, edited by Alan Poole and Frank Gill. American Ornithologists' Union, the Cornell Lab of Ornithology, and the Academy of Natural Sciences, 2002.

Scientists have been writing about North American birds for two centuries. In all that time, *The Birds of North America* is only the fourth comprehensive reference work covering the life histories of *all* North American birds. The series provides detailed scientific information, drawn from the research literature, for each of the 716 species of birds nesting in the United States and Canada, including owls. These authoritative monographs are available at university libraries in the reference section or online by subscription.

Eastern United States

Hawks and Owls of the Great Lakes Region and Eastern North America, by Chris G. Earley. Buffalo, NY: Firefly Books, 2004.

A handy, pocket-size field guide presenting thirty-three eastern species of owls and raptors. The species accounts are illustrated with color photographs, including useful comparisons of color morphs and juvenile plumages—images generally not seen in typical field guides. The tips for spotting and identifying each species are especially helpful.

Hawks and Owls of Eastern North America, by Donald S. Heintzelman. Piscataway, NJ: Rutgers University Press, 2004.

Heintzelman, a well-known raptor biologist and author, has included many of his own photographs in a new book that covers the same thirty-three species as Earley's work. This book provides basic information on habitat, distribution, food, nesting, behavior, migration, and population size, with additional chapters on owl conservation status and research.

Worldwide

Owls of the World: Their Lives, Behavior, and Survival, by James R. Duncan. Buffalo, NY: Firefly Books, 2003.

Jim Duncan is an owl biologist with the Canadian government agency Manitoba Conservation (and incidentally, the technical editor of the book you are reading right now). In his very readable, large-format book, he includes basic information about owl behavior and biology, as well as short species accounts, with range maps and photographs, for 205 owl species. This book is notable for the way Duncan draws on his extensive personal experience studying owls in the wild; its unique collection of essays about owl research written by other experts; and a fascinating section on "Owls in Mythology and Culture."

Biology and Conservation of Owls of the Northern Hemisphere: 2nd International Symposium; 1997 February 5–9; Winnipeg, MB, edited by James R. Duncan, David H. Johnson, and Thomas H. Nicholls. General Technical Report NC-190. St. Paul, MN: U.S. Dept. of Agriculture, Forest Service, North Central Forest Experiment Station, 1997.

At this landmark symposium, 143 owl experts from thirteen nations gathered to present their research on thirty-three owl species found in the Northern Hemisphere. This volume is a compilation of the papers presented at that meeting, on topics including owl biology, ecology, monitoring, habitat use, status, conservation, education, genetics, toxicology, diet, migration, and mortality.

Handbook of the Birds of the World, vol. 5, edited by Josep del Hoyo, Andrew Elliott, and Jordi Sargatal. Barcelona, Spain: Lynx Edicions, 1999.

The nine-volume series *Handbook of the Birds of the World* is an exhaustive source of information about every bird species ever studied by western scientists. Volume 5 includes the owls of the world. Like *Birds of North America,* this work can be found on the reference shelves of university libraries.

Owls: A Guide to the Owls of the World, by Claus König, Friedhelm Weick, and Jan-Hendrik Becking. New Haven, CT: Yale University Press, 1999.

This volume is the international equivalent of Paul Johnsgard's monograph on North American owls and is widely considered the authoritative scholarly work on owls of the world. It may be purchased with a companion CD showcasing owl vocalizations.

Owl-Watching

Guide to Owl Watching in North America, by Donald S. Heintzelman. Mineola, NY: Dover Publications, 1992.

How to Spot an Owl, by Patricia Sutton and Clay Sutton. Boston: Houghton Mifflin Co., 1999.

Both of these books are packed with tips for owl prowlers, including how to locate owls in the field, by day and by night, and how to identify them by voice and by field marks.

Owl Nest Boxes

Boxes, Baskets, and Platforms: Artificial Nest Sites for Owls and Other Birds of Prey, by Susan Dewar, Colin R. Shawyer, and Colin Shanter. London: Hawk and Owl Trust, 1996.

This book contains detailed information on the design, construction, and placement of artificial nest sites for owls and other birds of prey. Although the book focuses on owl species breeding in the United Kingdom, some of the species also occur in North America, and the tips are relevant for related species worldwide.

Owls in Myth and Legend

Owls in Folklore and Natural History, by Virginia C. Holmgren. Santa Barbara, CA: CAPRA Press, 1988.

If Jim Duncan's book hasn't satisfied your appetite for owl lore, try this unique compilation.

Field Guides

The field guides listed here cover more than just owls—they are guides to all the birds of North America. These general guides are included in case you are just getting started as a bird-watcher; any one of these books will make a good foundation for your bird library, and all include up-to-date information about owls.

All the Birds of North America: American Bird Conservancy Field Guide, by Jack L. Griggs. New York: HarperResource, 1997.

Birds of North America (Kaufman Focus Guide), by Kenn Kaufman. New York: Houghton Mifflin, 2001.

Birds: A Golden Guide, by Ira Gabrielson and Herbert S. Zim. New York: St. Martin's Press, 2001.

National Geographic Field Guide to the Birds of North America, 4th ed. Washington, DC: National Geographic Society, 2002.

A Field Guide to the Birds of Eastern and Central North America, 5th ed., by Roger Tory Peterson and Virginia Peterson. Boston: Houghton Mifflin, 2002.

Sibley Guide to Birds, by David Sibley. New York: Alfred A. Knopf, 2000.

Audio, Video, CD-ROM, and DVD Guides

You are far more likely to hear an owl than see it, so an audio guide is a very handy reference tool for owl-watchers. Some of these guides focus on owls only; others are regional or North American bird guides that include owls along with other birds.

Peterson Field Guides: Eastern/Central Songs, 3rd ed.
This CD includes ten owl species: Short-eared Owl, Eastern Screech-Owl, Long-eared Owl, Great Horned Owl, Barred Owl, Common Barn Owl, Great Gray Owl, Boreal Owl, Northern Saw-whet Owl, and Burrowing Owl.

Peterson Field Guides: Western Songs.
You might want to buy the western guide even if you live in the East, because this two-disc set includes all the owls of North America.

Stokes Field Guide to Bird Songs, Eastern, by Lang Elliott with Donald and Lillian Stokes.
Eleven owl species are included: Barn Owl, Eastern Screech-Owl, Great Horned Owl, Northern Hawk Owl, Burrowing Owl, Barred Owl, Great Gray Owl, Long-eared Owl, Short-eared Owl, Boreal Owl, and Northern Saw-whet Owl.

Audubon Society's VideoGuide to the Birds of North America. Vol. 3, *Alcids through Woodpeckers.* New York: MasterVision.

Available as a videotape or DVD, this is the third of a five-volume set that, taken together, depicts 505 different North American bird species. The narrated presentation combines photography, moving pictures, and bird sounds to provide tips for bird identification. Computer-animated maps show breeding and wintering ranges. The great thing about this video is seeing owls in action. The images of pigeons and doves, cuckoos, nighthawks, hummingbirds, swifts, trogons, kingfishers, and woodpeckers are a bonus.

Owls up Close. National Audubon Society, VHS video. 1991.
A fifty-five-minute videotape that presents eighteen species of North American owls, with basic information on their anatomy, physiology, and behavior.

Know Your Owls. Axia International, Interactive Multimedia CD-ROM for Windows.
This multimedia presentation helps you learn about the nineteen different species of North American owls through a combination of photos, full-motion videos, sound clips, and range maps. Includes descriptions of adults, juveniles, and color-phase variations.

Hawks, Eagles & Owls: Our Birds. Thayer Birding Software, CD-ROM for Windows.
Having trouble making an ID? Simply enter the bird's colors, size, habitat, or location, and Thayer's helpful ID wizard instantly shows you photos and names of all the birds that match your description. Also includes videos, maps, identification tips, comparisons of look-alike species, and recordings of vocalizations.

Bird Banding

www.pwrc.usgs.gov/bbl/
The U.S. Geologic Survey's Patuxent Wildlife Research Center is the home of the national Bird Banding Laboratory.

www.nabanding.net/nabanding/
The North American Banding Council is a non-profit that trains birders and offers certification.

Rare Bird Alerts

Birding.com
www.birding.com
This is a full-service website for bird-watchers, where you can find a state-by-state listing of rare bird alerts.

American Birding Association
www.americanbirding.org
This website also offers rare bird alert information.

North American Rare Bird Alert

www.narba.org/

The Houston Audubon Society sponsors the North American Rare Bird Alert (NARBA), a paid subscription reporting service that lets you know about rare birds that turn up in the United States and Canada.

Owl Pellets

A surprising number of vendors sell owl pellets. Here's just a sampling. (Listing does not imply endorsement of products.)

Pellets, Inc.

P.O. Box 5484
Bellingham, WA 98227-54841
phone: 888-466-OWLS
fax: 360-738-3402
website: pelletsinc.com/

Claims to be "the world's largest owl pellet supplier."

Hawks, Owls & Wildlife

701 Groveside Rd.
Buskirk, NY 12028
phone: (518) 686-4080
website: www.owlpelletkits.com

In addition to selling owl pellets and educational materials, this company runs a raptor rehabilitation center.

Carolina Biological Supply

website: www.carolina.com/owls/index.asp

This is a venerable source of biological supplies for educators, but you don't have to be a schoolteacher to order from them. In addition to owl pellets, the company also offers bone charts that can help you identify various species of owl prey.

Virtual Owl Pellet Dissection

www.kidwings.com/

Here's a fun website. Point and click at a life-size pellet to pick away the fur and sort out the bones onscreen. Select from among different owl species, and the contents of the pellets will differ. This site also offers a handy "bone chart" to help you identify the bones you find in a real dissection.

Owl Nest Box Plans

U.S. Fish and Wildlife Service

library.fws.gov/Bird_Publications/house.html

The U.S. Fish and Wildlife Service website has a section on "Homes for Birds," including owls.

Prefab Owl Nest Boxes

Here's a sampling of vendors that sell boxes sized for Barn Owls, Barred Owls, and screech-owls or saw-whet owls. (Listing does not imply endorsement of products.)

Bio-diversity Products
members.tripod.com/~Tommy51/products.html

Coveside Conservation Products
www.coveside.com/

BestNest.com
www.bestnest.com/bestnest/owl_houses.asp

Nest Box Cams

Cornell Lab of Ornithology
birds.cornell.edu/birdhouse/nestboxcam/
   Nest cams of several birds, including a Barn Owl.

OwlCam
www.owlcam.com/
   A camera that looks inside a Barred Owl nest.

FineBirdArt.com
www.finebirdart.com/owlcams.htm
   See Eastern Screech-Owls at this webcam site.

City of Cape Coral, Florida
www.capegov.org/owlcam/
   The city of Cape Coral is proud of its population of nesting Burrowing Owls.

Wildlife Rehabilitators

www.tc.umn.edu/~devo0028/
   This wildlife rehabilitation information directory has state-by-state listings.

Volunteer Opportunities

Project Owlnet
www.projectowlnet.org
   Northern Saw-whet Owls are migratory, but because of their night-flying habits, scientists don't know much about where these little owls go or when they travel. Project Owlnet was launched to fill this information gap. Saw-whet owl monitoring stations have been established throughout the Northeast, Mid-Atlantic, and upper Midwest, mostly at nature centers. Volunteers work at night, helping scientists net and band owls. The banded owls may

later be recaptured at other banding stations; by pooling the data, scientists can learn more about owl migration paths.

Breeding Bird Atlases

A Breeding Bird Atlas is a bird survey conducted within a single state. Most states have atlas projects. The goal is to document all the bird species that breed (rear their young) in the state. Atlas data is very valuable to wildlife biologists who are charged with monitoring changes in bird populations. The data can also be useful in land-use planning, since an atlas documents the distribution and abundance of rare and endangered species. Atlas volunteers look and listen for all kinds of birds, not owls exclusively—but atlas projects particularly need experienced owl-watchers. Different states carry out atlas projects at different times, so check with a local bird club to find out whether an atlas project is ongoing in your area.

Bird Studies Canada's Nocturnal Owl Survey

www.bsc-eoc.org/national/nationalowls.html

The volunteer-based Nocturnal Owl Survey, launched in 1999, is a project of Bird Studies Canada, a nonprofit conservation organization dedicated to advancing the understanding, appreciation, and conservation of wild birds and their habitats in Canada and elsewhere. Many of the better-known and long-standing bird surveys, such as the Breeding Bird Survey and Christmas Bird Count, don't do a good job of monitoring owls. The Nocturnal Owl Survey fills the gap. Volunteers drive along a predetermined route in spring, stopping at intervals to play recorded owl calls and listen for live birds responding.

The Birdhouse Network

birds.cornell.edu/birdhouse/

The Cornell Lab of Ornithology in Ithaca, New York, invites nest box landlords to submit data on the birds using boxes in their backyards.

Maine Owl-Monitoring Program

www.maineaudubon.org/conserve/citsci/owl.shtml

Maine Audubon and the Maine Department of Inland Fisheries and Wildlife operate volunteer-based owl surveys that are similar to Canada's Nocturnal Owl Survey. *Note:* Michigan and Wisconsin also conduct owl surveys.

SPECIES ACCOUNT INDEX

Also available in Stackpole's Wild Guide series

DRAGONFLIES

Cynthia Berger

Dazzling in appearance, idiosyncratic in behavior, dragonflies and damselflies have long captured the imaginations of nature lovers. This full-color guide takes you on a whirlwind trip through the lives of these intriguing insects, from their birth underwater, to their miraculous transformation into free-flying adults, to their elaborate mating rituals and globe-spanning migrations.

$19.95 • 136 pages • 60 color illustrations • 0-8117-2971-0

WWW.STACKPOLEBOOKS.COM
1-800-732-3669

Lincoln Township Public Library
2099 W. John Beers Rd.
Stevensville, MI 49127
(269) 429-9575